Beauty From Ashes

A Journey Of Faith

By Ali Joy

© 2018 Alicia Joy Whetstone Author

All Rights Reserved

Acknowledgements ....
6

Introduction ....
8

Chapter One ....
13

A Broken Road ....
13

Sorrow may last for a night but His joy comes in the morning ....
13

Chapter Two ....
37

Hope ....
37

Hope shines brightest in the dark ....
37

Chapter 3 ....
52

Adventure Awaits ....
52

The Unexpected Journey ....
52

Chapter four ....
87

Changing Tides ....
87

Learning To Surrender ....
87

Chapter Five ....
108

Discovering My Foundation ....
108

Finding My Faith In The Coptic Orthodox Church ....
108

Chapter six ....
133

Becoming Rooted ....
133
Choosing Orthodoxy ....
133
Chapter Seven ....
149
Abundant Life ....
149
Embracing The Fullness Of God's Love ....
149

Acknowledgements

First I want to give thanks to the Lord Jesus Christ, for He is the source of life and the foundation of my faith. It is His work in my life that I am delighted to share in the pages of this book. It is for His glory that I am recounting the greatness of His love and faithfulness throughout my journey of faith.

I want to also give thanks to everyone who has poured into my life spiritually over the years. There are by far, too many to name; so I will give a general thanks to you all and more specifically name only a few. The first on my list would have to be my Mom. For it was through her own deep faith that I have been the most encouraged and influenced. She passed on a great legacy of unwavering faith, unceasing prayer, and a devotion to live in complete submission and obedience to the Lord. It is my prayer that I can one day leave behind such a powerful legacy of faith to my own children; or perhaps simply in the lives of those who knew me.

Finally I want to give thanks to Abouna Michael and Mora and to all those within the Coptic Orthodox community, who have so lovingly and patiently walked alongside me in my journey. Thank you for introducing me to the foundation of my Christian faith and the beauty of this ancient Church. Thank you for adopting me into your families and fully embracing me as your own. I could not have written this book without you!

Psalm 19:14

"Let the words of my mouth and the meditation of my heart be acceptable in Your sight, O, LORD, my strength and my Redeemer."

Introduction

I have long desired to compose a book filled with the incredible testimonies of God's faithfulness in my life. To finally share in depth the transformative work of the Holy Spirit, within my life. How He has sustained, comforted and strengthened me in the midst of life's trials. Now is the time to pursue that desire.

It is amazing how much perspective is gained when looking back on our experiences. As a child I never could have imagined how many, amazing adventures, God would lead me through. Nor was I able to understand how He would use each experience to strengthen my faith and draw me closer to Him. In the midst of trials, suffering and heartache we are often unable to recognize God's Hand at work. We may feel as though He has abandoned us or perhaps we even feel He is punishing us. Yet, that couldn't be further from the truth. The truth is He is always with us, He will never leave us or forsake us. He is a loving and merciful Father who desires to redeem and heal us from the brokenness of sin.

I am no stranger to the brokenness of this fallen world in which we live. My life has been a series of battles with heartache after heartache, trial after trial. I know intimately what it is to be brokenhearted, to have a crushed spirit and to feel that you are a prisoner to circumstances beyond your control. My childhood was wrought with trials, sorrows and injustices of the fallen world in which we live. I grew up in poverty and every day was a struggle to find hope of a better life. Yet it wasn't the lack of finances, or living off of rice, beans, and the occasional cheap snack foods that I found difficult. For me the greater suffering was daily witnessing the crippling, captivity of poverty. Not just material, financial poverty, but poverty of spirit; watching the emotional bondage of poverty erode the hope and future of my family.

The captivity and brokenness in which we lived had roots going back for unknown generations. For we all carry with us those often unconscious habits and patterns of thought that we learned within our families. Growing up I knew very little of my parents childhood, nor did I hear the happy tales of how they fell in love and got married. On the contrary; I grew up wondering why they married and if there ever was a time where they were truly in love. For as far back as I can remember they were like two ships passing in the night, seldom interacting with each other. They were living separate lives yet residing in the same house, barely ever communicating. I honestly can't recall even one moment where they showed any signs of affection toward one another.

This was my family life, two parents living in the same home, yet never speaking lovingly. Never seeming to be on the same page about anything and not even sleeping in the same room. Although there are many things that remain a mystery about their lives, the brokenness of their marriage was no mystery; it was something I was all too aware of. The absence of love left a sorrowful imprint upon my heart, that I still feel today.

My Mom's relationship advice to us from a fairly young age was, don't marry someone just because they ask. Make sure this person is someone you want to build a life and family with. You see every time she offered this advice, she would tell us that this is advice she wished she had been given before getting married. Every time she offered this advice my heart would break a little, because in it I felt her regret. It revealed her suffering in a marriage that was lacking love and a firm godly foundation. It also taught me that suffering always goes deeper than the outward material circumstances. The suffering of my childhood went deeper than the financial poverty in which we were living. It was rooted in the spiritual and relational poverty of my parents marriage. That brokenness is what had us rooted in captivity.

Yet, in the midst of great suffering God was revealing Himself to me. He was directing my eyes toward heaven and unveiling the mystery of His deep love and the transformative power of the Holy Spirit. As I share a small portion of my life with you on the pages of this book, I write with a deep awe and gratitude for each step of my journey.

Though there are things I wish I had not had to endure, I would not change one single piece of my story. As I am now able to see, at least in part, how perfectly God has created beauty from the ashes. How He has transformed that which Satan meant for my destruction and has instead given me life, built me up and rooted me deeper in my faith. Throughout each trial He has revealed greater depths of His love, He has comforted me and strengthened my faith. He has so perfectly provided for my needs, and guided me from one season of life into the next. He has shown me that He is truly faithful and will continue His faithfulness in every season, trial and experience of life.

My faith is indeed the thing I am most grateful for, for without it my life would be but an empty shell. I am thankful for the firm foundation of my Christian faith. For growing up seeing the Lord reveal Himself to me through His Word, through the church and through my Mom's relationship with Him. I had the tremendous blessing of growing up within church, with a deep foundation in the Word of God, and an emphasis on prayer and intimacy with Christ. Some of my fondest memories of my Mom, were the early mornings she spent in prayer and Bible study. Her faith in Christ guided her daily and was clearly seen in her interactions with the world around her and in her reactions to life's trials. Although her marriage was full of brokenness, her faith in Christ and devotion the Lord guided her to honor the covenant of marriage in the midst of her pain and regret. She passed on to me a legacy of unwavering faith and deep intimacy with God. Were it not for God's thoughtfully laid foundation, for the beautiful example of my Mother's faith and her continuous prayers, my life would have turned out a whole lot differently.

As I have reflected back on my life I have discovered that I am now able to see beyond the brokenness. Although the pain and sorrow of my childhood remains a vivid memory. I have come to see things through a new perspective, that I guess comes with age and maturity. The brokenness was only part of the story, and only part of my parents marriage. There was also a great deal of strength, of faith and of love. Perhaps, not the perfect love of fairy tales, but the genuine love of endurance in the face of human imperfection. A love that I hope to live out in as graciously and effortlessly as my Mom seemed to. Though my guess is she struggled as much as I or anyone else does to walk in such love.

Over the years I have tried on many occasions to begin this project, yet the timing has never felt quite right. However, the more I have shared these testimonies with my friends, the more they have encouraged and challenged me to write a book. A book recording God's faithfulness and provision, a book full of the adventures God has taken me on through the years. So with their encouragement and the peace of God to begin, I have begun compiling the vast collection of His workmanship within me. I am finally sitting down to write that book, or perhaps the first of many books. May it all be for His glory and may it be encouraging to you in your own journey of faith.

"For by grace you have been saved through faith. And this is not your own doing; it is the gift of God, not a result of works, so that no one may boast. For we are his workmanship, created in Christ Jesus for good works, which God prepared beforehand, that we should walk in them." Ephesians 2:8-10

Chapter One
A Broken Road
Sorrow may last for a night but His joy comes in the morning

Psalm 34:18

"The LORD is near to the brokenhearted and saves the crushed in spirit."

As far back as my memories stretch, I can see the presence of God. I can feel His hands moving through each experience, and my heart fills with unspeakable gratitude for His deep love for me. As I reflect back on my childhood, teens and young adult life, I see and feel two parallel story lines. I can so easily recall the physical experiences and yet those experiences are only half the story. They are perfectly woven together with the often unseen spiritual life. Two realms of existence and experience that coexist, overlap and are mysteriously woven together. Though many are unaware of this spiritual life and the working of God within our earthly experiences, I can assure you it is very real. We read in *Ephesians 6:12 "For we wrestle not against flesh and blood, but against principalities, against powers, against the rulers of the darkness of this world, against spiritual wickedness in high places."* We live in a physical world where it can be difficult to grasp this concept of a spiritual battle. We all too often fix our eyes on the physical elements of our situations and experiences. Yet, I have learned and continue to learn that when we do that we fall short of the life God desires us to live.

When we lose sight of or are not aware of the spiritual wickedness and powers of this fallen world in which we live, we direct our pain, anger and frustrations on to people. Yet, as Christians God has given us the Holy Spirit to discern and unveil the spiritual battle going on all around us. He has called us into action as we see in the following verses also from: *Ephesians 6:13-18 "Therefore take up the whole armor of God, that you may be able to withstand in the evil day, and having done all, to stand. Stand therefore, having girded your waist with truth, having put on the breastplate of righteousness, and having shod your feet with the preparation of the gospel of peace; above all, taking the shield of faith with which you will be able to quench all the fiery darts of the wicked one. And take the helmet of salvation, and the sword of the Spirit, which is the word of God; praying always with all prayer and supplication in the Spirit, being watchful to this end with all perseverance and supplication for all the saints"*

Growing up my Mom modeled this and reminded us of these verses often. She inspired me to walk closely with the Lord, to be in the Word daily and to live in accordance to the Word of God. She was known for using the phrase "What Would Jesus Do?" long before it became highly marketed merchandise. She often reminded us that others view Christ through how we as Christians live our lives. The truth of her words has been confirmed through many conversations and experiences over the years and is forever imprinted upon my heart.

One of many experiences I remember quite vividly, was a discussion with my best friends Dad, who was not a believer. In fact he was rather strongly opposed to Christianity. I was around the age of seven or eight years old, and had invited my friend to church on multiple occasions. Yet, her Dad always refused to let her go. So one day I decided to ask him directly why she couldn't come with me. At first he resisted answering my question and asserted that as an adult he didn't need to give an explanation to a child. Now as a side note and just to give you a greater picture of this exchange, you should know that he was a very intimidating six foot six inches tall and a heavy set man. With an Irish temper and history of getting his way and having the last word. However, he didn't know how persistent and passionate I was that my friend should have the opportunity to go to Church and be introduced to Christ. So I continued to press him for an answer. I was finally rewarded with a great discussion on his view of Christians and why he did not want his children to go to Church. I was also given the opportunity to share my faith and confidence in the truth of the Bible and respectfully challenge his opposition to Christianity.

The core of his argument was that although the Bible may be correct, Christians don't live what they say they believe. He didn't want his kids to be taught by a bunch of hypocrites. He felt that in his experience Christian's talked a whole lot about the love of God, but walked in judgement, gossip and division. He questioned how any church or person could claim to truly represent the God of the Bible. Now, I have always been very introverted, and a bit shy, but the Holy Spirit was granting me courage as I had this conversation. I responded to his argument acknowledging that I am well aware that not everyone who calls themselves a Christian walks in obedience to the Word of God. Indeed, there are hypocrites who profess Christ but live as those without God. I also pointed out that the Bible is clear that all have sinned and fall short of the glory of God. So even as a Christian we wrestle with sin and are in no way perfect. Yet, if the Bible is truly the Word of God and the message within the Bible is true; then, wouldn't He want his children to know the truth. To grow in the knowledge of this truth and walk with the Lord that they may be saved.

I boldly asked him if he thought I was a hypocrite, or if I lived by the faith I professed. I would not have had such boldness were it not for the Holy Spirit. I was aware that my friends Dad was not the enemy. He was the human vessel that I was engaging with, but his opposition to Christianity came from a place of spiritual deception. I wasn't arguing with him or being disrespectful in my confrontation. I wasn't trying, to force my faith or even defend my faith. I was simply following the Holy Spirit's leading to establish open dialogue where I could share my faith, and learn his viewpoint. This conversation was not typical for me. As I mentioned I am an introvert and have always been quiet and somewhat shy. I also have a very strong tendency to avoid any and all conflict. However, I had been praying for my friend and her family regularly and the Holy Spirit prompted me at the right time to start this conversation. In the end my friend was not only allowed to come to church with me anytime she wanted. I also, gained the respect of her Dad and his heart was softened to the message of Christ. I still remember him telling me that I was the first Christian he had known who appeared to live by the faith I professed. That was a profound moment in my life, one that I will never forget. One that has repeatedly challenged me to truly live according to my faith.

His simple proclamation that he felt I lived according to my faith has been a source of inspiration to me over the years. Especially in times of conflict or injustice. I am reminded by his words, to truly live according to my faith. To walk in obedience to God's Word and love as Christ loves. I am an ambassador for Christ and people are watching and learning about Him through me. The question is, do I portray a true representation of Christ by how I live my life?

It was not long after that conversation that this challenge was put to the test. Now, we had some very interesting and unlawful neighbors growing up. At this time there was a family living next door to us that were incredibly challenging to love as Christ loves. For some reason, the son who was around my age, really hated me. I mean he just couldn't stand me and was constantly harassing me. His teenage sister was in a gang. His Mom was into drugs and prostitution. The police were frequently called to his house because of fights and other criminal activity. I wanted to be sympathetic to his situation but I also really wanted to feel safe playing outside with my friends.

Then one summer day I was walking home after swimming at my friends house. It was only three houses away, but his house was one of those three and happened to be right next to mine. On this particular day he gathered his sister and about twenty teenage gang members, to make that walk home impossible. Before I could even take in what was happening, I found myself surrounded by this gang of angry violent teens. I was barefoot in my swimsuit, and incredibly outnumbered. Yet I did my best to stand my ground and once the punches started flying, to defend myself. Of course I was no match for a whole gang, but thankfully they were mostly there to keep me from running. Most of the fighting was done with this neighbor boy. Still, it was not an equal match.

I don't remember exactly how my friend happened to find me but she and her Mom rescued me. They brought me back to their house where they called the police. The gang of course took off, and my neighbors hid inside their house till the police escorted me home to get my parents involved in the situation. My Mom came out, I believe my Dad was at work at the time, I don't recall him being there. Then the neighbor boy, his Mom and sister all came out at the request of the police. His Mom instantly started arguing with the police and denying that her kids did anything. Of course that wasn't believed because the police were all too familiar with this family. So she quickly changed her story saying that I had started a fight with her son and was lying about the gang of teenagers being involved.

My Mom's response was quite different. It perfectly portrayed her naturally quiet and loving nature. She didn't say much as the police officers were arguing with the neighbor. Despite their assertive declaration to the neighbor, that clearly I was the one who had been beaten up, was barefoot, in a bathing suit and no match for her son. No, my Mom, being the perplexing woman, of faith that she was, quietly informed the police and the neighbor that we would not be pressing charges. She then apologized for the police involvement and sent inside to change. Everyone then went on with their day. However, the story doesn't end there...

I remember longing for my Mom to console me and assure me that this kind of thing won't happen again, but I didn't get that comforting. Instead, my Mom had a conversation with me about forgiving and loving our enemies. Praying for them and blessing those who hurt us. Then just to enforce this message and give me the opportunity to walk in love and forgiveness, she had me bake cookies for the neighbor boy. Yep, you read that right, I had to bake him cookies! Initially, I was a bit upset by her response. I was harassed and then beaten and she expected me to bake cookies for my attacker, it didn't make sense. Although I was not happy about it and my attitude was not lined up with love and forgiveness. I followed through and baked the cookies. When I went to give him the cookies and extend forgiveness and a call for peace; the Lord softened my heart and gave me good laugh at his reaction. Apparently he also thought it was strange that I would bake him homemade cookies, and offer forgiveness. In fact he accused me, of poisoning the cookies! I told him I was a Christian and God calls us to forgive and love those who have wronged us. I also told him my Mom asked me to bake the cookies for him as a way of extending forgiveness just as God calls us to. He still thought they were poisoned, so he insisted that my little sisters eat some first just to make sure they were safe. When he saw that they gladly ate the cookies he accepted the rest of them. God used my act of obedience to my Mom's request, to extend love and forgiveness. God also used this peace offering to soften both the neighbors heart, and mine. I gained compassion for where he was coming from and accepted that he had never been shown Christ or what it is to live in love and peace. I also embraced true forgiveness for his attack against me. He learned that I was kindhearted and lived according to my Christian faith. God had truly softened his heart though this one simple act. He not only stopped harassing me, he wouldn't allow others in the neighborhood to harass me either.

I remember this event so vividly, although it happened long ago in my childhood. In fact I am almost daily reminded of the power of love and forgiveness that I learned that day. Although my Mom is no longer here to challenge me to bake cookies for those who have hurt me in some way. The legacy of her instructions to extend such love and forgiveness to those who have wronged me carries on. Through this profound lesson of love and forgiveness that my Mom so graciously and naturally modeled to me; I have discovered the freedom that comes through pouring out forgiveness. Through offering up love and choosing compassion over distain.

This particular experience is etched so vividly within my memory. Yet, it is the ongoing choice to walk in love and forgiveness that sets this apart from just a fond memory. It has become for me an aspiration. To make this not just a story I fondly remember, not simply a one time event; but to make it a way of life. A daily practice, an essential part of my being. This is no simple goal and aspiration. I know I have failed more often than I would care to admit. Yet I press on. I seek to love and forgive as Christ loves and forgives. I seek to follow in my Mom's footsteps of graciously and naturally choosing love in the face of injustice. It gets more difficult as the years go on. The hurts and injustices become more complex and seem only to multiply. Yet the freedom that comes from choosing to love and forgive is nearly incomprehensible.

The taste of such freedom encourages me to press on in this life long goal of choosing forgiveness, in the face of each new wave of injustice that enters my life. For years I struggled to reconcile my past, the brokenness of my childhood. Circumstances beyond my control, circumstances that appeared to hold me captive and rob me of my future. Yet, the Lord has delivered me from it all. He has freed me and established me; and continues to amaze me as He reveals Himself through each and every one of those experiences. The road to freedom is like that of the road to salvation. Long and arduous. It is an ongoing journey through valleys and trials, with suffering and hardships. Yet paired with victories and celebrations. Mountain top excursions that unveil greater perspective, and deep peace and joy that inspire you to press on and persevere through the next leg of the journey.

Growing up I was well acquainted with the valleys and hardships of life. Poverty, suffering and violence were all around me. I first witnessed a gang fight with guns involved when I was five years old. That experience was the first of many encounters with such brokenness and violence. I learned from a very young age to observe my surroundings carefully and have a plan in place to hide or escape a dangerous situation. Although I loved playing with my dolls and other normal girly activities, I was no stranger to wrestling. I became quite proficient in self defense, a skill that was applied often.

When I was about 6 1/2 years old we moved into a house on one of the most notoriously violent and crime laden blocks in our city. That was my home till I moved out at the age of twenty-four. Shootings, stabbings, rapes, prostitution, drugs, it all happened there. You never knew what threat you may encounter when you stepped out your front door. As the years went on the neighborhood deteriorated and the dangers increased. By the Grace of God I was never severely hurt. Though I did endure a few attacks and muggings, and faced plenty of verbal threats through the years. Though I have not lived a sheltered life and my childhood innocence was taken away far too soon. The Lord preserved in me a childlike spirit, a creative imagination and the heart of a carefree dreamer.

I wish I could tell you that my home and family were a place a refuge in the midst of all that danger. However, despite the deep faith of my Mom, our family and home life was just as broken, and pain filled as the neighborhood I grew up in. I honestly don't remember a time when my family wasn't broken, and my memories go back quite far. It seems we always struggled with the dysfunctional relationship patterns that had been passed down from previous generations. Although there was one difference, a difference I am eternally grateful for; we were being raised in the church. I am not entirely sure of my Mom's background with the church. Though I don't recall her mentioning growing up in the church, her faith and walk with the Lord was definitely the strength that held our family together.

Both my parents grew up in divorced families, with an alcoholic parent who was out of the picture because of their addiction and abusive behavior. My Dad's Dad had remarried so he grew up in a two parent household. However, there were many dysfunctional issues and both parents had a strong opposition to Christianity. My Mom grew up with her sister in a single parent home carrying with her the brokenness and dysfunction modeled by her parents. My Dad was introduced to the church as a child. Despite his parents opposition to Christianity, he was allowed to attend church, if only to get him out of the house for a bit. His relationship with my grandmother, his step Mom, was almost non-existent. I can't really go into any details on my parents childhoods as they both grew up in families where it was strongly advised not to discuss family issues with anyone! My parents did their best to pass that on to us as well, though I am certainly breaking that pattern by writing this book. In fact I broke it a long time ago having shared many of these stories with friends and mentors over the years. Then again I was never one for following traditions anyway...

What I can tell you is that my parents brought a whole lot of broken baggage into their marriage from all the pain and dysfunction that they grew up in. Many years ago, when I was just a child, I decided that I would break that pattern. I would learn from them but I would not repeat their mistakes. Sure I would make plenty of my own mistakes but I would not repeat theirs. For the most part, I think I have been successful in that goal.

By the time I was seven years old God had deeply captivated my heart and I was fully devoted to living my life for Him. By that time He had placed a couple things very deep within my heart. Things I have passionately prayed into from that young age till this present day. Those treasured areas of my heart include Egypt, marriage and family life and a life of service. From the age of seven I have sought to live my life in service to the Lord. It has been my prayer and desire to live a life fully devoted to Him. To live differently from the reasoning and ways of the world. Relying instead on the wisdom and direction of God to guide my steps.

As a child it seemed a simple prayer, and attainable goal. Yet over the years it became more and more difficult to walk out in. The closer I came to adulthood the more challenging that road became. I am so thankful my Mom trusted the Lord to lead me, and trusted me, to follow where He leads. The decision to live in accordance to the Word of God and avoid the ways of the world was greatly tested in my teens. I certainly didn't gain many friends by my choice. Yet God blessed me with a couple of wonderful friends who greatly encouraged me, not just in my faith but also in life. Now I should probably mention that another reason I didn't have many friends was because of the constant battle for self preservation. I was so very broken and had been dealing with so many adult issues and so many threats to my life and safety. Things my peers from church didn't know about or understand. It was extremely difficult for me to open up, to just be a carefree teenager. To have fun and not be overwhelmed by the possible consequences, of letting my, guard down.

As I briefly mentioned, my home life was not a place of refuge. In fact it was often a battleground, a very isolating battleground. I struggle even now to write about my home life. To be so vulnerable as to share what it was like growing up in my family. I hear the accusations of betrayal for daring to share anything less than a perfect and happy account of a Christian family. Yet it wasn't a perfect and happy family life, so to write it as such would be a lie. So as I attempt to finally share even just partially, what my home life was like growing up. I take a deep breath and say a prayer for guidance. It is important to me that the Lord guides my words, and that they come from a place of love and forgiveness. Not just an honest account of the brokenness, but a testimony of His healing and redemption from the ashes. I hold no accusation, bitterness, resentment or anger in my heart. The Lord has delivered me from the pain of my past. He has granted me the power to forgive and to love fully, deeply and unconditionally. As I open this window into my, home life growing up, I pray it directs your hearts to the great Love of our Heavenly Father. Because He was right there with me, holding me and sustaining me through the darkest of days. Just as He is with each one of us through every trial we endure.

So, what was it like in my home and family growing up? I am the second born child and the oldest of three girls, so that means I have an older brother and two younger sisters. I know most of you would understand that without the explanation. But since many people have known me for years without realizing I have a brother and two sisters, I figured I would state it clearly. I don't plan on sharing a whole lot of detail about my siblings, this is an intentional decision on my part. After all this is my story and my perspective on God's faithfulness and work in my life. Any stories involving my siblings will be written with the utmost discretion and tons of prayer! As I have already shared there was a great deal of brokenness in my family growing up. I certainly don't want to stir up past hurts or cause a rift in my relationship with my siblings. I love them dearly and pray for them often, and hope that they would find this book honorably written.

At one point in time things seemed fairly normal. Never really ideal or desirable, but certainly normal, whatever that is. However, somewhere along the way things shifted into complete disorder. My parents marriage was never one I wanted to emulate. Even as a young child I remember having discussions with my Mom about my views on how a marriage should be different from their relationship. I felt she was way to passive and compliant and my Dad far too dominant and yet so distantly involved and neglectful. We used to really argue over this topic. Yet as much as my Mom and I would argue or disagree on things, we would always discuss things openly and lovingly. She was the one person I knew I could be completely honest with and still be loved and respected by when we were not in agreement. My relationship with my Dad was very different... We lived in the same house but that was as far as our relationship went. We didn't talk unless it was a short argument or simple relaying of information. We did not see eye to eye on much and it seemed as though I upset him, simply by being me. *(Again, this is written from my perspective, this is how I saw our relationship, I felt as though I was not loved or accepted by my Dad.)*

There was a great deal of silence. Painful destructive silence. There was such a strong avoidance of conflict ingrained in my parents, that it cost them the restoration and healing that can only come from confrontation and discussion. Depression threatened to consume my whole family. Every single one of us battled depression at some level. Though it was never discussed. I once suggested counseling and quickly learned that was not an option my parents would ever consider. As much as I dislike conflict I have always been a bit confrontational. Or at least inclined to voice my opinion even when it is not asked for or wanted. Though over time I became much more inclined to follow in my parents footsteps and keep my mouth shut. It seemed that every time I voiced my opinion I would upset someone. Years of rejection and opposition to questions or opinions being voiced, lead me into what often appears a natural silence. It is an ongoing struggle for me to freely ask questions or speak up and voice my opinions. Even knowing I would always have my Mom's love, and respect; at some point after all that rejection or unwillingness to discuss things, you simply stop bringing things up. To this day I struggle to ask questions. I don't even think in terms of questions any more. I generally think in terms of observations, and am very guarded in sharing those.

On top of the painful silence that was rooted in self preservation. Physically, our home was anything but a home. My Dad had become a serious hoarder, to the point where we couldn't have anyone over. I lived with the daily fear that someone would report our parents to child services because of the living conditions. Our house wasn't big, but the rooms were a decent size, with the exception of the kitchen and bathroom. However, we had only narrow pathways through the house. The piles of junk my Dad had collected were mere inches away from the 9 foot ceilings. And once again my Mom was silent. She never confronted him about it, she never tried to clear things out. She just accepted it. The condition of our home, my Dad's hoarding, and a slew of other issues that were out of my control; lead to a very intense battle for perfection. I became obsessive about organizing, cleaning, and living minimally. I was striving to always do the right thing and never make a mistake. I needed to be in control, to excel in everything. I obsessively considered all possible outcomes and consequences of every action and decision I made. This often lead to a paralyzing fear of making decisions, no matter how small or simple they may be. I have come a long way in dealing with my anxiety and perfectionism over the years. Yet, I can still see situations where this anxiety and drive for perfection finds its way back into my life.

On top of my Dad's hoarding problem, the house was in serious disrepair from years of neglect. I remember repeatedly mentioning the need for a new roof when I was a child. My Dad dismissed it for years, because after all I was just a child. As a child and even today, one of my many hobbies was watching shows and reading books on home building, repair and design. Not only was the roof falling apart. We had foundation issues. Electrical issues. Plumbing issues. Flooring and plaster issues. And eventually, even had our gas was shut off, which meant no heat or hot water.

Living in northern Indiana, this lack of heat lead to very cold winters and the need to use space heaters. This also meant living with the constant danger of a fire igniting, especially, given my Dad's hoarding problem. Winter became a time I dreaded. My fears increased during the winter months because I knew of the potential dangers of using space heaters. I knew those dangers were significantly higher in our home, because of the mountains of papers, car parts, tools and containers of paints, oils and other compounds typically found in a garage or workshop. To this day I find myself uttering prayers of thanksgiving for God's protection during my childhood. Just the thought of our living conditions calls forth a prayer gratitude for my safety and the safety of my family.

Despite growing up in rather extreme poverty, I never had an issue with poverty itself. That is, from the financial side of poverty. The lack of finances is of course the definition most would use to describe poverty. However, it was the emotional destruction of poverty that was so utterly toxic. It was one thing to do without clothing, toys or even food. But to see the corrosiveness of poverty strip away the hope and perseverance of my parents was devastating. To see them surrender to the condemned state in which our home had fallen, as though there was nothing they could do to improve things is inexpressible. I can't find the words fully describe the state of brokenness in which we lived. I am not sure I even want to fully describe that part of my life. It is simply too painful to detail.

For years I suffered in silence. I cried myself to sleep. I battled fear. Fear within my home and fear going out from my home. Nothing felt safe. I had no one to talk to... Well, that's not entirely true. I talked with my Mom, though I never really felt reassured and nothing changed because of it. I felt alone and abandoned, unloved and discouraged. I battled for hope and often wrestled with the Lord. Questioning why He allowed us to endure such hardships? Why did my family have to be so broken? Yet, even in the midst of all my fears and struggles. Through the most unacceptable living conditions and the deepest pain. I clung to the Lord. He was my Rock and my Anchor. As much as I wrestled with Him, or cried to Him, I could not turn my back on Him. I could not blame Him or hold anger against Him. I knew Him far too well to do that. He had made Himself known to me. He had revealed the depth of His love to me. He had stepped in and rescued me every time my life was threatened. He had captivated me by His Word. I clung to His promises and prayed the Scriptures over my life, family and future. I prayed for deliverance, protection and guidance. I struggled to stand firm on the promises of God and to submit myself to His leading. I didn't understand, and don't fully understand why I had to walk through those experiences and hardships. But I did my best to walk in obedience to God and trust Him through those trials. What I learned from those trials, is that, He was and is faithful.

Though the Lord lead me down a path I have not always understood, and one that was often lonely. I have done my best to trust Him and follow where He leads. There were many times where the path I followed was greatly questioned. Times where it was even strongly advised against. To many it was illogical and almost reckless. Yet, as I have stepped out in obedience I have been continuously amazed by the journey. Though I have walked through many trials, the tides of hope came as I walked in obedience to a calling I didn't fully understand. As I surrendered my understanding, and embraced the peace of God's leading, I began to allow myself to relinquish control. I surrendered my plans and asked God to reveal His.

The road to freedom came through love and forgiveness. It was in learning to truly love my parents, as Christ loves them, that I was able to see their brokenness and pain. Through love my perspective changed. God melted away the years of hurt, frustration, anger and bitterness that had held me captive. I was able to forgive them for all the ways they had failed and hurt me. I was finally free. Free to accept them in their brokenness. Free to love them in their shortcomings and free, to establish a new path. To learn from the life I had lived and the pain I had endured.

Had I not endured those trials I may not have come to a place of such dependance upon the Lord, or developed such a deep hunger and desire for Him to guide my steps; without such sorrow I may not have experienced the intimacy of His presence so deeply? It was in the midst of those trials that my prayer life was established. In those hardships that I truly experienced His comfort, protection and provision. I may never fully understand why God allowed us to experience such hardships, but I do know that His ways are far greater than our own. I know that He is always with us. He loves us deeply and He desires to restore our brokenness. We live in a fallen world, full of injustice and sin and the consequences of our actions can be carried on through generations. Although I am all to familiar with the brokenness of this world, it was in the midst of great suffering that I was blessed to experience Christ's loving restoration. To feel His comfort, and to know His Presence and the truth of His Word. It was in, my Mom's faith and the example of her intimacy with Christ that I came to truly know and walk with the Lord. Because of her, I aspire to be a woman of deep prayer and faith.

Just as my Mom lived out her life in prayer and unwavering faith, I too pursue such precious intimacy with the Lord. I have devoted myself to prayer and to live my life by the guidance of the Holy Spirit. It is a life long journey and I have had plenty of failures along the way. Times where I grow weary or frustrated. However, it is in those times of frustration or exhaustion that I look back on the hardships of my childhood. In looking back I remember the faithfulness of God to deliver me from those trials. I reflect on the countless times the Lord has answered my prayers. Guided my steps, and healed my wounds. I remind myself of His leading, His guiding me into a life of service. A life devoted to seeking and following where He leads. I praise Him for His wondrous works and the fulfillment of my prayers and desires.

Throughout the years the Lord has granted me many talents and skills, and as a child I had many dreams and plans for my future. Though, I am most known for desiring to be a wife and mother. In middle school I began praying about my future. How I should pursue developing my talents and skills in the way of a career. In high school I continued to pray over this and received more counsel and advise on the subject than I ever really wanted or asked for. Yet despite the wisdom of the counsel and advice that was given, I never had peace to follow it.

I had always thought I would go to college and pursue some kind of degree. That was certainly in line with the counsel I was given. Yet, the more I prayed into this plan the more confused I became. I couldn't settle on a specific field of study. I could see the benefits and possibilities of my options. But every choice lacked peace. As I prayed into each possible option, I felt the Lord leading me down a different road, calling me to set aside the wisdom of this world and trust Him for something greater. Thankfully my parents were accepting of this and didn't pressure me to follow the normal path. Though it was much harder to find this acceptance, from my peers and youth leaders in the church.

At the time I found it very frustrating, I mean I was simply trying to follow where God was leading me. It's not like I was being rebellious and irresponsible. I was just not heading off to college like my friends.

Of course now I can see where they would be a bit concerned. Especially those who had a small understanding of my living situation and home life. They wanted me to secure a path to a better life. Yet, here's the thing that I so greatly admired about my Mom. She knew that the best path to a better life was to follow where God was leading me. She trusted that I could hear and know God's voice. She also believed that the better life may come from not following the wisdom and normal pattern of the world. But may come in a completely different and unexpected way. I am eternally grateful for her support and trust in me to walk in obedience to God's leading.

My Mom knew a thing or two about prayerfully doing things differently than what is expected or considered acceptable. You see she had decided to homeschool all four of us at a time where homeschooling was almost unheard of. Being homeschooled from Kindergarten all the way through High school, I had the freedom to explore many areas of study. As an independent student with a love for learning, it was a great fit for me!

I taught myself how to read around the age of four and have been an avid reader ever since. Growing up I would visit the library weekly always bringing home a backpack full of books. Not just the age related books my friends were reading. I was known for selecting books from outside the children's room and from a wide array of topics. Even today, I love reading and have an ever growing library of my own. I enjoy learning new things and gaining deeper insight into areas of interest. Some would even call me a jack of all trades. My love of learning was perfectly paired with my heart to serve. Though I didn't always realize this, especially when I was trying to figure out what to do after high school. I never had a passion for a specific career, which was frustrating at the time. As I considered and prayed about career paths I felt the Lord calling me into a life of ministry and service.

As I mentioned before, I have always been known to have a strong desire to be a wife and mother. It is something that comes very naturally for me. I truly have a life time of experience caring for children and running a home. Because of this many were counseling me to pursue a degree in Early Childhood Education or some other related field of study. However, I never felt lead to pursue a degree. Though I have done plenty of independent study in this area, it has never been a goal or desire of mine to formally study and establish a career in this field.

Despite the counsel of many to pursue a college degree that would secure a more financially sound career, I have chosen to follow the Lord down another path. I feel the need to clarify that although I have chosen not to go the route of college, nor to pursue a specific career. I am not opposed to that path should the Lord lead you down it. I simply believe that we need to devote ourselves to prayer in all things, and allow God to guide our plans. For many college is a part of that plan, yet that was not His plan for me.

It is not about choosing a better path or a higher road. It is all about walking in obedience, to the Lord. As I have walked in obedience to God's leading He has shown Himself faithful and granted me peace every step of the journey. He has also granted me steady employment from the age of fourteen, mostly in childcare. Though I have also had the incredible experience of serving Him in full time Missions, both in the States and abroad! My time in Missions is a truly amazing part of my journey of faith and I can't wait to go into more detail on how the Lord opened that door. To share with you the wonderful adventures I experienced during that season of my life. But we are not quite there so you will just have to wait... Don't skip ahead, you may miss out on some important details of the journey!

Chapter Two
Hope
Hope shines brightest in the dark

Psalm 71:5

"For you, O, Lord, are my hope, my trust, O, LORD, from my youth."

It is in the darkest of times that the hope of Christ seems to shine the brightest. Of course you have to open your eyes to see the light...

My battle with depression began around the age of ten. Yes, you read that right, at ten years old I was battling depression. Now since I grew up in a family where we didn't discuss such things and only went to Dr.'s for serious illness or regular vaccinations; I was never officially diagnosed with depression. Although I was never officially diagnosed, I can assure you I was indeed battling depression. Since I never had a professional diagnosis, I am not sure if there were any imbalances or disorders and such that were feeding the depression. What I do know is that between the ages of ten and fifteen we faced many hardships and the loss of many loved ones. It was a very dark season of my life and depression nearly overpowered me. It is not easy for me to share this part of my life, in fact this is the first time I have ever shared this part of my life with anyone. Yet, I feel the need to share this vital part of my testimony with you now. I am sharing because I believe there is much hope and encouragement to be gained through sharing how beautifully the Lord delivered me from my battle with depression.

If you are battling depression I strongly encourage you to seek counsel. Talk to your Doctor or find a mental health professional to speak with. You do not need to face this battle alone. I pray for those reading this who are battling depression that you may find deliverance and freedom from your battle. May you reach out for help and encouragement to find the path to victory, and may the Lord grant you full healing and restoration.

Those five years of my life were the climax of brokenness. They also happened to coincide with puberty, creating the perfect formula for depression. During that time things at home shifted from somewhat normal into indescribable chaos. I suppose it happened gradually as most things do. Though looking back it seems as though things transformed practically overnight. We were hit with a great many trials during that season of life and though I was only a child I was painfully aware of the hardships we were walking through.

Winter of 1991 was a season of loss. I can't even recall how many deaths we experienced in such a short amount of time. It seemed as though every time the phone rang we were hearing of yet another close friend or family member who had passed away. Of the numerous deaths, there were two deaths that stand out from the others. Two deaths that greatly changed our lives and had long lasting affects on our family. That winter we lost our most beloved Grandmother after watching her battle Alzheimers. We also endured the traumatic sudden loss of my brother's best friend, in a car accident.

As a child it can be extremely traumatic to experience the death of a loved one. That winter we became well acquainted with death. There was indeed no sheltering us from its presence. The loss of a friend our own age heightened our awareness of our own mortality. Though it is always a challenging thing to come to terms with the death of a child, as a child myself it was even more difficult to process. The reality of my own mortality and the knowledge that tragedy can enter one's life so easily and unexpectedly added to my battle with fear.

The sorrow experienced from this kind of loss is life altering. I witnessed the deep brokenness, the denial, anger, fear and many other stages of grief. His parents, brother and each member of my family were experiencing these emotions and stages of grief with added intensity because his death was so sudden and unexpected. During the grieving process I became keenly aware of how fragile and precious life is. As someone who naturally has the heart of a mother and caregiver I was inclined to feel responsible for everyone's well being. This made an already challenging experience harder for me to walk through. I didn't know how to comfort everyone. I didn't have answers or words of wisdom that would bring healing and peace. His death was so sudden and unexpected. It left us all in a state of shock and deep sorrow.

Sorrow was a constant companion that winter. The loss of my Grandmother was particularly heart wrenching. Perhaps it was because I was the first granddaughter. The fact that we shared a birthday. Or maybe it was because I shared her creativity and we loved using our talents to bless our friends and family. It may have been the long process of seeing her health decline. Or simply the depth of love I held in my heart for her. All I know is that loosing my grandmother truly broke my heart.

It was painful to watch Alzheimers steal away her memories, her vibrancy and passion for crafts, gardening and us, her grandkids. The heartache continued as we saw her physical health deteriorate rapidly. Our once amazingly strong, fun and active Grandmother soon became a fragile shell of her former self. Yet somehow, the sorrow of her death was also paired with the relief that her days of suffering were finally over.

I greatly missed the nights spent at her house, playing in her yard, helping her with her garden, and exploring her craft room... She taught me many things; cooking, baking, sewing and how to crochet. She is also the one who first inspired me to write. It was her own love of writing and incredible book collection that captivated me for the written word. We also enjoyed shopping at the mall together and going out for lunch dates. Or simply enjoying a visit at her house. I remember she had what seemed like hundreds of little porcelain figurines that my siblings and I always loved playing with. Her bathroom was full of sea shells she had collected from her time living Florida and her home always smelled of roses. These are the sweet memories that are ingrained within my heart. When I think of my Grandmother I think about her love and all the wonderful times we spent together. Though I wish we would have had many more years together, I am blessed to have so many joyful memories with her.

 Wouldn't it be wonderful if all our memories were as joyful... Of course that is not the case. Nor was enduring the sorrow of so many deaths the only hardship we were facing. It was also during that season of my life that my Dad became an obsessive hoarder. My Mom transitioned from being a full time homemaker into the main breadwinner. And the dangers of our neighborhood increased rapidly. There were a lot of difficult changes and adult issues that I was drawn into and made to deal with. The weight of these burdens and responsibilities weighed heavily on me. I struggled under the weight of my own unrealistic expectations. I battled the fear of letting everyone down and losing control. I felt responsible for everyone's well being and yet I was unable to fix all the brokenness. In addition to my own expectations I carried the weight of many household responsibilities. I had always seemed very mature for my age, and independently took on so many responsibilities around the house. This lead my Mom to rely heavily on me for a great many things after she entered the workforce. Unfortunately, she also had a tendency to turn to me as an outlet for her concerns. Often sharing issues she should have been discussing with my Dad. This greatly added to my burdens and battle with depression.

Because of this, I was keenly aware of our lack of finances, delinquent bills, limited groceries, deteriorating home and my parents marital discord. Yet I was completely helpless to change any of it. However, that doesn't mean I didn't try to improve things, in fact I was often trying to improve things. I used the knowledge I had gained from books and other observations to tend to many household repairs. I attempted many times to clear away the mountains of junk my Dad was collecting. Though that only lead to more tension in my relationship with him and the piles always returned. I was working fairly often even at the age of ten, babysitting for neighbors or families from church. I would use my income to cover my own toiletries and often buy dinner or groceries for the whole family. I also did my best to help my sister's in school, and I did the majority of the cooking and cleaning from the age of ten.

My siblings and I were all very close when we were young. However that changed over the years and was especially challenging during this season of our lives. My brothers grief came out mostly in the form of anger. Sadly he directed much of his anger at God and ultimately turned his back on all things Christian. The rest of his anger was often directed at us. I didn't really care for that and having developed my wrestling and self defense skills I didn't have to deal with the physical anger for long. I still remember the look on his face when I pinned him on the floor! Although that put an end to the physical aggression, he quickly found a different way to inflict his anger upon me. His verbal abuse was nearly impossible to escape and caused far more emotional damage, deepening my battle with depression. Of course looking back I am able to recognize it was all part of his own grieving process. He was hurting too. He wasn't just being a jerk. He was a child and teenager like myself, learning how to deal with the weight of negative emotions.

As for my sister's... My sister's and I all shared a room which was originally thought to make us grow closer, and strengthen the sisterly bond. That decision and line of thought came from our Dad, and proved to be unsuccessful. I mean really who puts, three, hormonal girls in the same room? I can laugh about many of our crazy antics now, but there were some really dramatic fights that took place in that room. One minute we were best friends, the next aggressive competitors or arch enemies. And one thing we all have in common, is the fact that we are highly passionate about our beliefs or opinions. However, we don't always share the same beliefs and opinions, so you can imagine the drama that ensued.

As I mentioned before I have always been one to follow the rules and weigh the effects and consequences of my choices. This of course developed mostly from the chaos and brokenness of my home life. Although this is generally a good thing, when paired with pride and obsession it is quite destructive. I never went through a defiant rebellious stage, that just wasn't me, but I have certainly battled the sin of pride. I boasted of my "righteousness," my obedience to abstain from so many sinful actions, while looking disdainfully upon others, for their sinful choices. This of course did not go over well with my siblings, friends or really anyone. Thankfully the Lord does not leave us unaware of our sins and is patient and merciful in leading us to repentance. I was certainly in great need of His mercy and patience.

One of the ways the Lord convicted me of the sin of pride was through the book of James. There He specifically, convicted me of the need to control my tongue, walk in humility, be merciful and seek the Lord for wisdom. He showed me that while, by all appearances, I may be walking in obedience, I was sorely lacking in humility and love, which revealed the sinful condition of my heart. The Lord revealed to me that my motivation for doing the "right" thing was not always about seeking Him and His Righteousness. But was often about seeking the approval and praise of others. I felt unloved, and unwanted. I felt as though I was a burden and inconvenience to both family and friends. Because of this I was desperately trying to prove my worth and earn love and acceptance. Thanks be to God I was pursuing that love and acceptance through trying to be responsible and godly. Otherwise my life may have been filled with much greater hardships and far more serious consequences. Sadly I have so painfully seen this happen in the lives of those I love.

Looking back now, I believe the Lord, also lead me to the book of James because it is filled with encouragement to persevere in the midst of great trials. He knew just how difficult the coming years would be. During those five years battling depression I turned to the promises within the book of James and many other Scriptures for encouragement and strength. I learned how to gain more control over my tongue and walk in greater humility, thus leaving the conviction of sin to the Holy Spirit. Instead of judgement I began choosing prayer and compassion. I was not perfect in this of course, but the Lord began His work of prayer and compassion in me. Although I still battle this today to some extent; by the grace of God I am growing. I am much quicker to walk in love and prayer and leave the conviction of sin to the Holy Spirit. I earnestly seek to walk in love and humility and prayerfully give counsel only when asked for.

It may seem strange to hear, but I am actually incredibly thankful for that dark season of my life. That's not to say I want to endure such suffering and hardships, I really do not desire to walk through the pain of those experiences again. However, it was during those darkest of days that God strengthened my faith. Stripped down my pride and clothed me in the humility that comes from experiencing my utter dependence upon Him. This of course is an ongoing lesson and not a one time accomplishment. It was also in my brokenness, that God revealed the depth of His love for me. Awakened hope, established a rich prayer life, and captivated my heart with the promises of Scripture. Therefore I am grateful for that season of my life and all that I have learned through those trials.

It was also during this time that I became keenly aware of the spiritual battle that was raging all around me. A battle where Satan was desperately seeking my destruction and eternal separation from Christ. Yet, by the end of those five years God had drawn me out of the hopelessness, fear, frustration, bitterness and anger that had held me captive. He had established hope and forgiveness. Given me vision and passion for my future, and filled my heart with compassion and love for my family.

I remember quite vividly my last battle with the fiery darts of depression. They came upon me with such force right when I thought I had finally overcome the weight of depression. I was bombarded with such dark emotion and intense feelings of despair and felt the devil pressing me to give up and end my own life. It was a truly terrifying experience. I was shaking and crying in my bed, and began praying, "Lord have mercy, Lord please help me I can't go on. I don't want to live like this. Lord I need You." And in that moment, I physically felt as though His arms embraced me. I heard Him say so clearly, that He loves me. That He is with me and He has a plan and a bright future for me. He said, "Alicia, you are loved and my plans for you have not yet been fulfilled. Rest in Me." I was instantly covered in His peace. All the fiery darts of the enemy filling my head with depression vanished.

That was the end of my battle with depression, though it was not the end of my families hardships or my own struggles. Circumstances never really improved in fact they got worse. Finances became a greater struggle, and the condition of our house continued to deteriorate. Relationships with my siblings fell apart. Yet the peace of God dwelled richly within me through it all. My faith increased and my pride decreased. I devoted myself to prayer and held on to the Word of God for encouragement, hope and direction. I learned to entrust my family into God's Hands and establish healthy boundaries in my relationship with them. I was no longer trying to fix everything or carry the load of responsibility for everyone. I began actively writing and developing my artistic abilities. I was becoming very active in the Youth Group and serving in the children's ministry at church. I was also blessed to participate in a peer counseling course through the church. Through which the Lord helped equip me to process the hardships I was facing at home, in healthier ways.

As I finished up high school I began fervently seeking God for an opportunity to pursue a life of ministry. He began unfolding a journey that to this day, continues to amaze me. This incredible journey of my faith is what is inspiring me to write this book. To share the wonderful work of the Lord, offering up praise for His great love and faithfulness. May it be an encouragement to you in your own journey of faith. May it inspire you to view the hardships and trials of this life through a different lens.

I know as I look back over my life I continue to be amazed by the love and faithfulness of God to use every experience as preparation for better loving and serving those He brings into my life. He has certainly granted me my prayer for a life of service. One where I am continuously amazed by the intricacies of His workmanship and how He leads us from one season into the next.

As He lead me out of my battle with depression He was strengthening my faith and increasing my desire to live a life of service. I was earnestly seeking him for direction for my future as I poured myself into my studies and serving in the children's ministry at church. As I began developing my writing and artistic abilities, I began considering using those talents within a career or life of ministry. Though God had granted me victory over my battle with depression, I still had a long journey ahead of me to build up my hope and confidence for a better future. I still felt restricted by my circumstances, and burdened by the weight of my responsibilities at home. Though I was learning to place those burdens before the Lord in prayer it was a slow process. Yet, I was beginning to see His plans unfolding in my life.

 Although I did not grow up in the Orthodox Church, I am very thankful for having grown up in church. Not only within church but with a Mom who was truly devoted to the Lord and living her life in accordance to the Word of God. When I was first introduced to Orthodoxy as an adult I found it truly amazing how the Lord had shaped my own faith and understanding of Scripture in such a way that it felt like discovering the roots or foundation of my faith. It wasn't difficult for me to embrace Orthodoxy, though it was difficult for me to reconcile my Protestant background and relationships, in choosing to become Orthodox.

I had grown up in church, where the Lord had been so faithful in developing my faith and guiding me in my walk with Him. Although I had certainly discovered many areas where my beliefs didn't align with the church I had grown up in, it was hard to walk away. It was hard to close that door, to leave that chapter behind me and officially choose to become Orthodox. In many ways it felt like a betrayal. It was as though I was turning my back on my Protestant friends. That in choosing Orthodoxy I was diminishing their faith, declaring it to be corrupt or false. I was afraid of pride creeping back into my life. Of my perspective towards my Protestant Christian friends changing because I had chosen Orthodoxy. I was also worried that I would once again be cutting myself off from my siblings because of my pursuit of God and this time it may not be repairable. I know that God should always come first. Although that is certainly my desire, having lost both of my parents, my siblings and their families are the only family, I have. The thought of severing those already delicate relationships is heartbreaking. These are just a few of the thoughts I wrestled with after discovering Orthodoxy. I knew I had a decision to make and I even knew exactly what I should choose. Yet I found myself once again struggling to trust the Lord in the midst of this internal battle.

It's interesting how when we are in the midst of the battle we are often unable to distinguish the root of our problem. And yet we continue to wrestle, when in fact what we need to do is step back and gain some perspective. For me much of that perspective has come as I stepped back from the battle of decision. Though it wasn't really a conscious choice of mine to take a step back. It came about after years of wrestling with God. I was living a distracted busy life trying hard to hold onto my own understanding and vision for my future. I was clinging tightly to a bunch of what if's and the pathway that God had used in leading me out of the bondage of my childhood. Yet as I look back I can see that as much as I was praying, I wasn't really surrendering myself and my future to the Lord. This had left me utterly exhausted and in need of a very drastic change. One that God in His great mercy and love prepared for me in His perfect timing. However, before we get into that part of the journey we must first go back to the beginning of the pathway that lead me out from my childhood home and the trials of that season of my life.

Beauty From Ashes

Chapter 3
Adventure Awaits
The Unexpected Journey

Proverbs 16:9

"The heart of man plans his way, but the LORD establishes his steps."

I was working as a Nanny, caring for a good friends nephew and niece. That position was going to be coming to an end soon so I was praying about my next steps. I had never shared with their Mom my desire to pursue missions and a life of ministry. In fact I had held that desire pretty close to my heart not voicing it to anyone but the Lord. However, one day as we were in the car talking I began to tell her that I was praying about this long held desire. I hadn't even gotten the words out of my mouth before she finished my sentence with, "You're praying about going into missions." Then she tells me about a missions organization she had just learned about and offers to help me get information and look into my options! It was such a beautiful confirmation to my spirit that God was moving and leading me in this direction.

After researching this missions organization I discovered they offered many locations around the world. I began narrowing it down and contacting my top five locations for further information. I was growing with excitement to pursue the missions training schools they offered. I was eager to set out in following my dream of serving the Lord in the Nations! Of course there wouldn't be much to write about if everything came together easily... So once again I was about to face more challenges. Challenges that would test my devotion to God and strengthen my faith in new ways.

Despite having requested information from five locations I only heard back from one location, Nashville TN! Now, something many of you may not know is that just as God had placed Egypt on my heart, He had also placed Nashville on my heart. Or at least captivated me with a desire to live there one day... I don't think I mentioned this before, but I am a dreamer. I have always been a dreamer and God has always spoken to me through my dreams. In one such dream there was a beautiful tree lined driveway out in the country somewhere. It was a place that felt like home and a place where young people were being discipled and strengthened in their faith to reach the world for Christ. Little did I know at the time that Nashville was where I would find that beautiful tree lined driveway. I was about to experience first hand the vision of young people being sent out into the nations with the hope of the Gospel. I was about to discover a place that will always feel a bit like home.

As I read over the information packet this missions base had sent me, my excitement grew. I knew this was where God was calling me. However, not everyone shared my excitement. In fact when I first shared my desire and the information with my parents they were completely against it. Why you may be asking? Well, there were probably a few reasons, but their strongest voiced opposition, had to do with finances. Specifically, the fact that I didn't have any. You see, the missions organization was calling those who join them to raise their own financial support. Now, my Mom, in particular, had a huge problem with this concept. She was adamantly against asking people for money, no matter what the cause or need. She was also reluctant to let me leave the nest even though I was in my early 20's.

So, now I had this calling burning deep in my heart, it was a desire to serve the Lord and minister to people. It was a good desire, yet I was convicted by the Scriptural command to honor your Father and Mother. I did not have their blessing or support to step out in this calling, and so I waited. I waited and prayed and tried hard not to push the idea on them. My job as a Nanny came to an end. Despite my efforts to find another job where I could save up to cover the cost of the missions training and outreach, I was 100% unsuccessful. I was officially unemployed. For the first time in my life I was struggling to secure a job that would bring in enough money to cover my responsibilities and save for this training. I was confused and frustrated. I poured out my frustrations to the Lord, asking Him over and over why? Why would He place a life a ministry in my heart and lead me to this missions organization, yet, not let me have the support of my parents? Why was He not letting me earn the financial provisions needed, to cover the tuition and outreach expenses? I had been working since the age of 14, I had been providing for myself and helping to provide for my family and now I could barley provide for my own personal needs.

As a warning, this next little section may be quite controversial as it is full of some very personal and deeply emotional experiences, however, after several writing attempts I feel this should be included.

On top of this personal challenge and the struggle with being unemployed, things began to get bumpy at church. Now I had always been very involved in church. I was there any time the doors were open and I had been regularly serving in the children's ministries for years. However, the differences between my faith, the understanding and Christian beliefs I personally carry, and those of the church I was attending were becoming much harder for me to ignore. In fact there were some things happening that I just could not stand behind. Looking back now I see this as a pivotal point in the journey of my faith. In many ways it was the start of my journey towards Orthodoxy. Of course at the time I didn't realize that. I had yet to encounter the Orthodox Church, so lets not jump ahead to that part of the story, just yet.

So how were things getting bumpy? Well, as much as I have tried to leave this part of the story out, I just keep coming back to this experience and how intricately woven into my journey it is. This next little bit goes into some family details that many people in similar situations would try to keep on the down low, so to speak. It is rather difficult for me to write about this because it involves my sister and some of her life choices. I certainly don't want to over share or upset her by sharing, yet, I do feel this should be included. So I prayed hard about it and asked for her permission before writing the following section.

My sister and a couple of other young women in the church sadly became pregnant outside of marriage. They were all around the same age, late teens just entering adulthood. This was an extremely difficult and heartbreaking reality. One my whole family and the families of these other young women, had to navigate through. It was also something that couldn't really be hidden from the church congregation, nor do I think it should have been hidden. However, the way these young women were treated by those in the church was in my mind unacceptable. Now don't get me wrong, I am in no way condoning sex outside of marriage. Its wrong. Its sin, and that should not be sugar coated or glossed over as though it's no big deal. However, these young women, my sister included, were in desperate need of the love of Christ. They needed to be drawn toward repentance and shown forgiveness. They needed godly counsel. They needed a safe place to face the new direction and responsibilities their choices had brought them. Unfortunately, the church didn't offer them love, forgiveness or godly counsel. They were cast out, gossiped about and pressured to quickly marry the father's of their babies in order to set things quote, right.

Now, you may be saying, "But of course they should marry these men they had chosen to be so intimately involved with. They need to own up to their sins and accept the consequences of their choices." Yet, I ask you, "Do two wrongs make a right?" Are we as Christians truly counseling someone to remain in an ungodly relationship? To enter into the sacred covenant of marriage on the foundation of their sin? Is this really leading them to repentance or simply providing the appearance of making things right? If there were no children involved, if it had only been discovered that they were sexually involved with their boyfriends; would you counsel them to get married so their sexual relationship would be acceptable? Or would you be counseling them to turn from their sin and end these relationships?

These were teenagers on the verge of adulthood. They were young women who I imagine were hurting deep inside and were desperately seeking to be loved. I am not sure how things should have been handled, or what counsel should have been offered. What I do know is that they were harshly treated, unwelcome and the counsel to quickly marry did not lead to their repentance. Watching my sister walk through this season of her life, seeing her continue to go further away from God and the church was heartbreaking. Seeing the painful consequences of her sins unfold in the destructive relationship she was in was painful. Yet seeing her condemned, shamed and gossiped about from those within the church, to me was in many ways far worse. Knowing she lumped me in with them, and felt judged by me simply because she knew that I disagreed with her choices was hard to swallow. We had always been close growing up, I adored her. Though I know I could have done a better job of showing my love, especially in my teens. Yet her sin drove a wedge between us and it broke my heart to feel her distance herself from me. She knew that I wasn't going to simply call her sin a mistake or poor judgement. Or anything other than sin, and that broke our once close friendship.

She knew I did not approve or support her sinful choices, but I honestly never felt anything but grieved by her choices. My love for her never changed because of her sin. I did however, struggle with knowing how to convey that love for her without any doubt that I utterly opposed the sinful lifestyle she was living. Many of my prayers for her expressed this struggle and through the Scriptures God reminded me of His unconditional love and complete forgiveness. A love and forgiveness that is extended toward each one of His children, my sister included. I found myself convicted by Romans 5:6-8 "For while we were still weak, at the right time Christ died for the ungodly. For one will scarcely die for a righteous person—though perhaps for a good person one would dare even to die— but God shows his love for us in that while we were still sinners, Christ died for us." As I meditated on these verses and the incredible love of God, I chose to focus on loving my sister and loving my nephew. I didn't have to pretend that I approved of sex outside of marriage, in order to love her. Nor did I have to constantly lecture her about sin and reminder her of Scripture, in order to make it clearly known that I did not in any way support her sinful choices. It was my responsibility to love her and pray for her. So I tried my best to extend love in practical ways and cover her in my prayers.

My protective big sister nature really rose to the surface a lot during that season of life. Especially when some in the church went so far as to condemn my sweet baby nephew because he was conceived outside of marriage. To many he was merely a fleshly consequence of a sinful, sexual act. A bastard child with no purpose but to bring shame upon my sister for the rest of her life. I however, entirely disagree with that line of thinking. I had no problem letting anyone who dared speak such things know exactly what I thought of such ungodly hate filled thinking. My nephew, along with every single person that ever existed or will exist is created in the image of God and is given life by God! We are all created and given life by God Himself and no other. He is the one knitting us together within our mothers womb. He has a plan and purpose for each and every one of us. A plan that is not voided by the circumstances of our conception in situations of intentional sexual sin or a forced sexual assault.

Again let me make it clear I am in no way saying that sex outside of marriage is acceptable or anything other than sin. It is sin. It is disobedience to the Lord and His teachings. As a Christian I do not approve of any sexual relationship outside of marriage. I am also not ignorant to the science behind how babies are conceived. Yet the Word of God is pretty clear in the Scripture when we read, *"For You formed my inward parts; You knitted me together in my mother's womb. I praise You, for I am fearfully and wonderfully made. Wonderful are Your works; my soul knows it very well... Your eyes saw my unformed substance; in Your book were written, every one of them, the days that were formed for me, when as yet there was none of them."Psalm 139:13-14 & 16.* Though we are all conceived through a sexual act, it is God who gives life. God chose to give life to my nephew. My nephew is a precious gift from God and I can't imagine life without him. I even see God's mercy and redemption in his birth. Though of course there were also, many destructive things that came from my sister's choice to sin, my nephew is not one of them.

Seeing these young women, my sister and the other two whom I had also known for several years, being vilified and cast out from the church truly broke my heart. As Christians we should be lovingly leading people to repentance and redemption. Not vilifying them for their sins. Yet that is exactly what was done with these young women. They were viewed as harlots, a leprous poison in the church. Their children were viewed to be merely a consequence of their sin, and by some an outward punishment to shame them for their sins. It angered me to see the beautiful sacrament of marriage being diminished, used simply as a false atonement for their sin. As though appearing righteous is the same as being righteous. The concern wasn't for their repentance but simply for appearances. Things needed to appear appropriate. Thus if they were pregnant or had children they needed to also have a husband, or never show their face within the doors of the church. It was easier to cast them out then it was to walk alongside them, lovingly guiding them down, the long and arduous road of repentance and healing.

Obviously this is still a sensitive and passionate topic for me. I now have multiple nieces and nephews, most of which have sadly been conceived outside of marriage. There are times where the heartache I feel for both of my sister's choices and lifestyles is so overwhelming. I try not to even think about it. Though that is next to impossible, since I would have to remove them from my thoughts and I could not put them out of my thoughts even if I wanted to. I love all three of my siblings. I love all of my nieces and nephews, and I wish I could tell you that they are all walking closely with the Lord. Living out the Christian faith our Mom modeled for us. Yet that is not the case. In fact it is often wondered by people who know of our different paths in life, how I came to be living so differently from them. Or them from me; given we all grew up in the same family.

I admit I have wondered the same thing at times. However, one thing I have learned over the years is that we all process life experiences differently. It is by the grace of God that I am who I am today and yet as I write that I pause. I pause because in saying that it seems as though I am saying that His grace has not been extended to them. Yet isn't God's grace given to all? Truly we grew up in the same family with the same exposure to the church and the Bible. We all witnessed our Mom's faith and devotion to the Lord. Yet we have not all chosen to follow the godly instruction we were raised upon. This brings up yet another issue

I have had with the Protestant background I grew up in. Far too many believe they have the authority to interpret the Scriptures and make applications according to their own understanding or emotional desire. Both of my sisters if asked would tell you they are Christians, and have been for many years, nearly their whole lives. I don't claim to know the heart of any one, nor am I able, to speak to whom God will receive into eternity with Him, myself included. Yet I know full well the dangers in picking and choosing which Scriptures you will embrace and which ones you will leave out because they don't sit well with you.

A Christians life will reflect Christ, there will be visible growth and spiritual maturity as we are conformed into His likeness through the Holy Spirit. Our obedience and submission to live according to the Word of God is essential to our Christian faith. The transformative power of the Holy Spirit in my siblings lives is often difficult for me to see. Yet I continue to pray for my siblings just as our Mom continuously prayed for each one of us. That we may truly know the Lord and walk in the way of salvation.

Despite the heartaches of seeing my siblings live more secular lives, I am aware that life is a journey. The development of our faith is a process that continues throughout our whole life and is not a one time decision. Over the years I have certainly seen growth and maturity in each of their lives, just as I have seen in my own life. Yet my concern for my siblings lays in the Protestant belief of, once saved always saved. The idea that all you need to do is confess to being a sinner once. Ask the Lord to forgive you and live in you, then your salvation is secure. As wonderful as that belief sounds, I don't see it backed up Biblically. Though it may be widely held as truth by many within the Protestant Christian faith, I believe it leads to many spiritual insufficiencies.

Although I grew up with this teaching of instant salvation, it never sat well with me. Aside from the weak Biblical support for such a belief, the resulting tendency to coast through life as a nominal Christian is quite startling. The sacred reverence for the Lord seems to have been replaced, by the Jesus is my best friend philosophy. This leads us to an apathy towards repentance and sin. It also leads to many living a secular lifestyle despite identifying themselves as Christians. A pattern I feel I have so clearly seen played out in the lives of my siblings.

There was another situation that arose within the church I was attending at that time which really was a breaking point for me. Again looking back I see this series of events as a catalyst moving me toward a new outward alignment of my faith. One that would unite me with the internal workings of my faith by bringing me into the Orthodox Church of which my Christian faith truly aligns. Although I actively served in children's ministries within the church I was also very involved in the College young adult Sunday school class. One of the things I loved about this class was that there were much deeper discussions. Yet that also revealed more clearly the areas where my Biblical understanding and Christian faith varied from those of my peers and the church. Now even though these discussions would often stir up conflict of our beliefs, I didn't generally speak up to argue or question those things I disagreed with. Remember I am an introvert and at the time was battling many fears and insecurities. I did my best to avoid any and all conflict.

Anyway, at this time there was a shift in leadership within the young adult Sunday school class. With that shift came a very alarming discussion one Sunday during class. Now a discussion in and of itself is not the problem, all things can be discussed. Yet when you proclaim something that is 100% sinful as being perfectly acceptable, even my strongly introverted self will rise up in protest. One of the young women had brought a friend or boyfriend to church with her, who was an actively practicing Wiccan. Though he also, claimed to be a Christian... First off, What? Anyway, the discussion went something like, is it possible to practice both, to be Christian and Wiccan? Now you would think the answer to that would be fundamentally clear across the board of Christianity. "No, you cannot be both." However, after discussing it for a short time the Teacher said something along the lines of, "Of course, its fine to explore and experiment with different belief systems, and have a combination of practices." Jaw dropped, to the floor! Am I still in church, was I some, how transported to an alternate universe? How can I be hearing this, and better yet why is no one speaking up and confronting this falsehood? I was in complete shock. After recovering slightly I tried to speak up and confront this lie, however, I was shut down immediately.

I walked out of class in a state of shock and confusion. I then shared this news with my Mom, who, always wanting to see the good in people, said that maybe I just misunderstood what was said. Well, that didn't go how I expected... So I figured I would talk to the previous teachers about it, however, they were out of town. On top of this horrible teaching, and everyone just blindly accepting it as perfectly in line with Scripture. The new teacher asked this Wiccan guy to lead the next weeks, ice breaker. I was outraged by this. I went home from church and looked up every verse I could find that talks about witchcraft. Along with verses talking about serving two masters and anything else closely related to this topic. I wrote out detailed notes and highlighted all these verses in my Bible prepared to give an unscheduled lesson on the subject. I refused to be silenced! This needed to be addressed!

However, I did not get my chance... In fact that next week I walked out of the class in tears and physically shaking because, the ice breaker this guy was doing was a numerology "game." The purpose of which was to predict what day of the week you are more inclined to be tempted to sin. Everyone was participating and oohing and awing over how accurate it was. I was horrified by the Spiritual ignorance of my peers and friends. After interrupting my Mom's Sunday school class and sharing everything with her through my tears, we brought the issue before the Pastor's. It was in their hands now...

However, it quickly became a, he said, she said, it must have been a misunderstanding of what was said, kind of situation. I was ready to leave the whole church behind. However, my Mom calmed me down and asked me to give the Pastor's time to pray about it and address things. So instead of leaving the church, I simply withdrew from the Sunday school class. People began gossiping about why I was no longer in Sunday school and what "happened" that fateful Sunday that I walked out of the classroom. For the first time in my life I felt the sting of being the topic of everyones gossip. The good thing about that was I could now relate to how my sister felt being the center of cruel gossip.

I was confused and upset with how things were being handled regarding the whole situation. Yet I didn't know what else to do about it. I loved this church. I loved the people. However, it was as though a veil was being lifted from my eyes. I was seeing so many things happening there that were not inline with Scripture. And now because I had spoken up, my faith and character were also being called into question. My Mom encouraged me to hold my head high and devote myself to prayer for the situation, the ministry of the church and especially for the young adult class. So I did my best to follow her advice and for about 6 months I spent the Sunday school hour in prayer in the narthex of the church. I ignored the gossip, and refused to get into any discussions on what did or didn't happen. The Pastor's worked to restructure the young adult class. Part of that restructuring meant the person who was giving and allowing these unbiblical teachings and practices was removed from teaching. Unfortunately, I later learned this was only temporary.

As I prayed for the church I also continued to pray for my parents hearts to be opened to my pursuing the missions training. In addition to praying for my parents blessing, I was also asking for God to somehow provide the finances. It took a full year of prayer and being unemployed. Yet somewhere along the way the hearts of my parents softened and they began to see that this was something God was truly calling me into. As I gained my parents blessing to pursue this training I also began learning the importance of community within the Body of Christ. It was a humbling experience for someone like myself who has always been so independent. I was learning that I needed to allow others to come alongside me to help me. To partner with me in this journey and life of ministry. This lesson like most is not a one time lesson, it continues to be repeated at deeper and deeper levels along the way.

After my parents gave their blessing I sat down with my Pastor to discuss my interest in this missions organization. I sought his permission to share with the church and ask for their financial support. During our conversation he voiced a few concerns about the missions organization. Like my parents he brought up the issue of raising financial support as his biggest concern. I expressed that I was well aware of this element of joining this organization. I had done my research and was comfortable with the information I had read. I showed him the paper work and he gave his blessing.

He asked me to prepare a short presentation and allowed me to share in front of the whole church about my desire to pursue this missions training. Over the course of that year of waiting and praying I had also sought the prayers of a couple in the church. They had been overseeing the young adult ministry before the unbiblical teaching incident occurred, and were like second parents to me. After sharing my plans with the church they offered to drive me down to Nashville when the time arrived. Within one week of sharing my plans with the church, I had raised ALL of my tuition and outreach expenses. Over $6,000! I was so blown away by the support and generosity of the church congregation.

I soon set off to begin my missions training and though I didn't know it at the time, I was about to embark on a whole new chapter of my life. One filled with an abundance of adventure. Answered prayers. New friendships and dreams unfolding before my eyes in ways I never could have imagined possible. It was the beginning of a journey that had long been desired. One I had unknowingly been preparing for through the trials of my childhood and adolescence. You see it was through those trials, through the suffering and struggles that God had been equipping me, strengthening me and developing me. He had prepared me for all that would unfold in the coming years. The foundation of my childhood, the hardships I never understood were a preparation for a life of ministry. I just didn't realize it at the time.

It was a strange feeling leaving "home." Embarking on an uncertain journey. Following a long held desire that had for so many years been just a dream and a prayer. Yet the moment the car pulled into that beautiful tree lined driveway, I so clearly recognized from my dreams. I knew I was fulfilling my destiny. I knew I was coming home. In this new season I was about to experience an overwhelming abundance of the Love of God. To be so sweetly broken by the greatness of His plans for my life. I was being released from the chains of my heartache and the trials I had endured. The Lord was performing a deep transformation within me throughout that training school and overseas outreach. One that would leave me forever, ruined for the ordinary.

During the lecture phase of my training school I wrestled most with accepting the abundance of love God was showering down on me. I felt so unworthy of the answered prayers, fulfilled dreams and outpouring of love I was experiencing. Truthfully, I still struggle with feeling unworthy of the incredible love and blessings God has bestowed upon my life. Life had been a struggle and a constant battle for so long. I wasn't accustomed to the love and support I was now receiving. I didn't know how to embrace this new abundance of provisions. I was overwhelmed by the love and friendships God had brought into my life within the missions organization I was now a part of. It was a whole new challenge for me, but one I quickly embraced.

I was soaking up this new found awareness of God's presence. I was devouring the spiritual nourishment of the teachings and life within a community of believers. It was an incredible season of biblical teaching. Group intercession, and times of worship. Having godly fellowship, accountability and ministry opportunities was a whole new experience for me. Of course it also had its challenges. I suddenly had a ton of roommates. All younger, and all coming from varied backgrounds and levels of maturity. I thought sharing a room with two little sister's, was difficult, I had no clue how easy that was in comparison to dorm life.

That first training school was such an incredible season of growth. It was full of testimonies of God's provision and faithfulness, not just in my life, but in the lives of each of the staff and students involved in the school. We were standing with one another encouraging and building one another up in our faith. Battling in prayer for one another and speaking truth and hope over one another. Of course when you have a group of believers who are pursing God, seeking to know Him more and to make Him known to others, you will also encounter many spiritual attacks. These came in many different forms and we were not always aware or prepared for them. We were all facing various spiritual attacks. Satan wanted to prevent us from growing deeper in our faith and from taking the Gospel to the nations. For some it came in the form of finances, or physical illness. Battles with addictions and issues from our pasts. Or even relationship issues among our classmates and staff. Yet we were not facing these battles alone. We had the support of so many prayer warriors. We were being constantly covered in prayer by the amazing staff, our families and churches back in our home towns, the guest speakers and one another.

As we got closer to the outreach phase of our training, we began praying over locations. Because of the size of our school, we were going to split into three outreach teams. Each team going to a different country. If I recall correctly, the staff had been praying over locations first, they then presented us with the three outreach locations. At that point we needed to pray over the locations and choose our first and second choice. The staff were also praying over which students and staff members should be a part of each outreach team. So after each of us submitted our choices they formed the teams and announced the big news to the class. To my amazement and sheer delight, Egypt was one of the outreach countries.

Despite my excitement over the possibility to finally experience Egypt first hand, I struggled to believe that God would actually grant me my desire. I was beyond amazed when I was chosen to be on the team going to Egypt! I hadn't even shared my heart for Egypt with anyone before that announcement. I was overjoyed when I learned that God was bringing me to the very nation He had placed within my heart as a young child. It was once again a very personal and intimate confirmation that I was walking within His will and following His leading.

As we began our outreach preparations I soon discovered many of my supporters had concerns over my going to Egypt. Although I was very excited for this opportunity I could understand their concerns. I had my own concerns as well. I had never traveled outside the US before, and knew the possible dangers of going into a Muslim country for the purpose of missions. I wasn't going into this outreach unaware or unprepared. Though I later learned that many thought that was the case. I knew the risks of missions work in such a nation, yet I firmly believed in the Lord's leading and His divine protection. My concerns however, were not related to the country we would be entering.

My concerns were for the team that I was going to be a part of. Our team had some difficult relational challenges to say the least. We also had two guys from our team leave the school right before the outreach. Honestly that was a big relief to me since both of them had been seriously wrestling with God and personal issues throughout the lecture phase. However, that left our team with only 3 guys in total, one of those being our school leader. Now for those of you who may not be aware, this absence of guys, placed our team in a rather vulnerable position. We were going into a male dominant Muslim country where simply being a woman leaves you vulnerable to many dangers. Having male teammates provided us with some level of protection, and sense of security. So losing two guys from our team right before outreach increased our vulnerability. Yet, God's plans are always so much greater than our own, and He certainly did not forsake us when our plans changed. In fact, I firmly believe our outreach team was composed of exactly the right people for those two months of ministry. As difficult as it was to lose two members of the school and team right before outreach it really was the best situation for all involved.

De-boarding the plane in Egypt was a very surreal experience for me. Just as I felt that entering the tree lined driveway of the missions base in Nashville felt like coming home, this too felt like coming home. There was something so familiar about it all and yet at the same time so unknown and foreign. There was so much to take in and process. It was exhilarating and overwhelming, and then there was this whole jet lag thing I had only ever heard about. That first week is a bit of a blur. However, I do remember staying in a somewhat sketchy hotel, that honestly inspired me to do a whole lot of praying. So I guess even that was a positive experience. One thing I clearly remember was our assignment on our first full day. I remember this assignment, because it seriously made me question the sanity of our leaders. For our first full day in Cairo we were split into small groups and sent out into the city on a scavenger hunt of sorts. It was intimidating and yet very empowering. It showed me that once again God was using my childhood experiences as preparation for the days ahead. Growing up in an environment where I needed to be mindful of my surroundings and cautious of men, certainly prepared me for traversing a Muslim country.

Over the course of those two months in Egypt God was stretching me and continuing His work in my life. He was gently calling me out of my comfort zone and into the fulness of who He created me to be. I was learning to walk in boldness and humility. I was learning how to encourage and challenge others in love, and I was learning the power of a prayer uttered in faith. Prayer was the foundation of our outreach. It was the core of our ministry and it was the healing of our team. As I briefly mentioned, our team had some difficult relational issues. In fact, these issues nearly lead to our whole team being sent home. Thankfully that did not happen! Our leaders confronted the issues head on and challenged us to walk in love and unity with one another. They urged us to walk in forgiveness and repentance towards one another. Challenging all of us to fully submit ourselves to the Lord and the ministry He had called us to in Egypt. As we began humbling ourselves and laying aside our differences, we began to see God move. He was moving both in and through us.

From the very beginning of the outreach I had partnered with a couple of the other young women on the team. We had committed to pray together daily and hold each other accountable in our struggles. The time of prayer, confession and encouragement we shared daily is one of my most cherished memories from this outreach. It was the key to loving our teammates through our differences and struggles. This devotion to prayer also prepared our hearts to love the Egyptian people. The love God gave us opened many doors to build friendships and share our faith. The Lord was moving mightily during those two months. We were blessed to serve in orphanages, hospitals, schools, villages and everywhere in between. As much as we were ministering and blessing others, God was also ministering and blessing us. He was continuing His work of redemption in each of our lives.

One of the lessons God was teaching me came through an unpleasant experience with sickness. I have always battled with feelings of unworthiness and the obsession to be perfect. Tirelessly trying to prove myself useful, strong and capable. I fear being a burden or a failure or somehow limited and restrained from whatever perceived success I have envisioned for myself. So when sickness prevented me from going out for ministry holding me hostage in my hotel room within close proximity to the bathroom. I was very upset. I felt as though I was letting everyone down and failing not only the team, but failing God. After all I was in Egypt for ministry and now I was stuck in bed unable to minister to anyone. Or so I thought...

I passed in and out of consciousness throughout that day of illness. Over the course of the day the Lord was laying many things on my heart. At times I think I may have even been hallucinating or perhaps I was having visions. Either way, there were some very lifelike experiences of situations and needs that urged me to pray. At one point I was shaken awake with such a fierce urgency to pray for my sister. To pray for protection of her life and for healing. Another time I was moved to pray for another outreach team. Several more times for members of my own team. Throughout that day when I felt my weakest and wrestled with

God about missing out on ministry, the Lord was speaking to me. I felt Him reminding me that He is not limited by my weakness. His strength is in fact more clearly seen in my weakness. He was showing me that even in my weakness I can turn to Him in prayer. That even in my physical limitations I am always able to choose prayer. He was teaching me that ministry is not always about works. Ministry begins in submitting ourselves fully to the Lord and devoting, ourselves, in prayer.

After our team returned from ministry that day I began hearing testimonies of how God had been moving. Those testimonies were perfectly aligned with the prayers I had been urged to pray over them that day. Upon returning to the States I learned that the prayers I had prayed for the other outreach team were also specifically addressing experiences they were facing on their outreach. Yet the most powerful testimony of God's Hand at work through my prayers that day, came when I learned that my sister had been admitted into the hospital with a severe kidney infection. She was admitted to the hospital the very same day I was awakened to pray for her. My prayers for the protection of her life and for healing were in accordance with her needs. Needs I was unaware of till my return. She was told that if she had delayed going to the hospital she may not have survived. The Holy Spirit clearly urged me to pray for her at that precise moment. Through that experience I learned that God can move through me even in my greatest weakness and that prayer is a powerful ministry.

Following that first missions training school I returned "home" to my parents house for a month before heading back to Nashville.

Over the course of the first school I had decided to attend a second school at the missions base. This would allow me to pursue coming on staff full time if that was where I felt the Lord calling me. That month between schools was probably the longest month of my life. It was so difficult to return to my family and the conditions of life I had left behind. Although I had grown and changed greatly during the five months I had been away, little had changed at home. Returning to those conditions left me feeling isolated, discouraged and out of place.

During my five months of training and ministry I had discovered freedom. The Lord had not only revealed more of Himself to me, He had also revealed more of myself. I had begun to discover the person He had created me to be. I couldn't return to the life I had lived before. I wasn't the same person. Although, mysteriously, in many ways, I was the same person I had been before. Though I was a more confident and authentic version of myself, if that makes any sense. You see I had found the freedom to become more of my true self. I was and still am, learning to embrace who God has made me to be. I am learning to live an authentic life. I am discovering my voice after many years of keeping quiet. I am uncovering my talents and learning how to walk confidently in my true identity. I no longer identify myself with the poverty and brokenness of my youth. I have truly learned to embrace my identity in Christ.

After experiencing such freedom I was eager to return for that second school. Although I had no idea what new challenges I would face. The next five months brought many challenges that were often very uncomfortable. These challenges offered me plenty of opportunities to grow in my faith. Finances for this second school did not come flowing in as easily as that first one had. I had the verbal support and excitement of many people as I pursued further missions training. However, the financial support was much more challenging for me to secure. Despite this struggle, God was moving in other ways. He was confirming His calling upon my life, and building my faith. One of the strongest encouragements was seeing how He had completely changed my Mom's heart. Giving her excitement towards my leaving home to join this missions organization. Before she had given her blessing but was at the same time trying to guilt me into returning home. After sharing with her all the ways the Lord had been working in me during the school and outreach she saw how life giving this calling was. She knew I was walking out in the will of God and became fully supportive of my new life in missions. Although finances were still very tight for my family, she sent money regularly and had truly become my biggest supporter. Although her financial contribution was small her prayer and advocacy, made her my biggest supporter.

God was once again faithful and the finances slowly came together. The slower pace of raising financial support provided me with an opportunity to grow, not only in my faith but also in humility. It is a very humbling experience to raise financial support. The school was full of these humbling experiences as I was constantly being taken outside my comfort zones. Throughout those five months I was challenged to develop many often ignored skills that my introverted self would rather continue ignoring. The focus track for this second school was leadership. For an introvert who battles insecurity this was incredibly intimidating. Yet, I knew it was exactly where I was supposed to be.

It was during the two month outreach in South India that I made the decision to come on full time staff at the missions base in Nashville. I was fully devoting myself to missions long term. I wasn't entirely sure what God had in store for my future but I knew He was leading me. He was very clearly answering my prayers for a life of service. There were many financial challenges that came with going on staff. The students are not the only ones to raise their financial support, all staff are required to raise their own support. It is a fully support based missions organization. Though it was intimidating and full of challenges, God continued to provide. He was faithful to grant me the desires of my heart as I delighted myself in Him and the plans He was unfolding before me.

My time in missions was marked by many heartfelt desires being fulfilled. One of the greatest desires of my heart was Egypt. After having experienced two months among the Egyptian people on that first outreach, my desire for this nation and people, was growing stronger by the day. I was praying, dreaming and seeking God about my future among this people and nation I had grown to love so much. I was eager to return to Egypt and to dive into whatever ministry God had for me within this beautiful country. Egypt was a place God had planted within my heart as a child and I was full of anticipation for how He would establish a long term ministry there. The challenge was discovering what that looked like. How would it all unfold? What was my role to be within the

Egyptian community? When would I get to live amongst these people who had completely captivated my heart, who felt so much a part of me?

As much as I wanted to return to Egypt, I did not want to return alone. That first outreach had taught me just how difficult it can be for a woman to live in a Muslim country. Surly it made more sense for God to provide me with a husband first. Or at least a team of others who shared my love for the Egyptian people. That made sense right? It was clearly the safest way to go about missions in a Muslim country. After all that is not the best place for a single woman to travel alone, much less live there alone. Right? Although I was trying to make my own plans and they seemed very sensible to me and especially with my supporters. God had other plans...

While I was co-leading an outreach in Costa Rica God spoke very clearly to me that He didn't want me sitting around waiting and praying for a husband. He didn't want me trusting in the covering and security of marriage or even a ministry team. He wanted me to place my trust fully in Him. To find my security in Him and to lay my plans down at His feet. About a month later I found myself juggling two roles. I was staff and I was a student. I was once again a student, however, this time I was also working on staff. This meant continuing to work part time while attending the school full time. The goal of this school was preparing for long term overseas ministry.

Throughout the school I was learning about successful long term, overseas missions. I was also discovering the more challenging side of support based missions. Finding people who believe in the calling you are so confident and passionate about. I was preparing to move overseas, to serve in Egypt for an unknown timeframe. Possibly even making a long term move overseas. Then my life got turned upside down, and my plans began to unravel. My once faithful supporters began pulling back, voicing concerns about this plan. Some began questioning the doctrinal views and the leadership structure of the missions organization. Stating that they believed it was negatively influencing my beliefs and Christian faith. Yet all of that paled in comparison to the news I was about to receive. One night after arriving back at the base from a class held in the city, I received a phone call that forever changed my life.

I always turn my phone to silent when I am in church or a class. So I had missed the numerous calls from my sister earlier in the evening. As I began walking back to the dorm I turned on my phone and discovered several missed calls. And a message in my voicemail... I stopped to listen to the voicemail. My eyes began to fill with tears as I learned my Mom had been taken to the hospital unresponsive. My phone then rang once more as my sister called to tell me the heartbreaking news that our Mom had passed away from a massive stroke. I remember falling to the ground with a loud wail and tears flowing down my cheeks. I was shaking and wailing and trying to process this devastating news. In one phone call my life seemed to break into a million pieces. I was completely shattered.

I don't remember how that phone call ended. I think I said something along the lines of, I will come home as soon as I can...

I was in complete shock. Yet, I do remember my small group leader and school leader coming over and holding me. Trying to comfort me. That is when once again the Lord showed just how personal and loving He is... Out of the fields came this stray dog that I hadn't seen in a few weeks. A dog I had often enjoyed giving affection to while I was out for walks and prayer. My school leader tried to shoo the dog away, but I pulled him in for a hug. I said, "No, let him come. God brought him here to remind me that He is always with me." So there I sat in the gravel parking lot hugging this dirty stray dog. Being held by two amazing women and bawling my eyes out with the most pain filled tears I have ever known. Yet, in that place of utter brokenness God was gently comforting me, directing my eyes toward Heaven.

I got on a plane early the next morning, but the week that followed is mostly a blur. My Mom's death was sudden and unexpected. We hadn't been aware of any serious health issues, so this left us all in shock. By the Grace of God we began walking through our grief, one foot in front of the other, one moment at a time. I felt His presence and peace through every moment of that week, and the months to come. It was a very difficult week. I was honestly quite taken aback by some of the things people felt they needed to say. It wasn't necessary to voice how disappointed my Mom must have been that I hadn't gotten married or given her grandchildren. That instead I was off chasing after childhood dreams, and leaving my family to struggle. I still can't believe those things were spoken, and at her viewing of all places. Yet those were far nicer things than what was spoken of my siblings and how their life choices were a far greater disappointment to our Mom. Now before you pull me aside and give me a talk about forgiveness, let me explain why I am sharing this particular memory. I assure you I have forgiven them.

I share this experience for a couple of reasons, but before I expand on that I need to share what happened in response to these things being spoken. As I shared from the very beginning of this book, my Mom was a woman of great faith and prayer. My Mom worked in retail and she was greatly loved and respected by her co-workers and regular customers. These hurtful words spoken carelessly by someone from the church were quickly confronted from a most unexpected source. It was my Mom's co-workers and regular customers, who spoke up and challenged these comments.

Now I don't know their backgrounds, if they were Christians or not. However, they knew my Mom. When it was suggested that her children had disappointed her, they quickly spoke up and rebuffed that claim. They shared how she always spoke of each and every one of us with great pride and deep love. They informed me that she was just sharing an update with them about my plans to move overseas for missions work. They told me she was incredibly proud of the young woman I had become. It was such a beautiful testimony of how her faith was known through the ordinary daily interactions of her job. It was also a comfort to hear how she shared her love for us with them.

So why do I share this? I share this because we all face similar situations. Situations where someone challenges our faith or the path we have chosen in life. Or situations where they simply say or do something that is hurtful. Yet, when we are truly living according to our Christian faith, walking in obedience to the Lord, the truth will be known. I also share this because as a Christian I am not living my life to please people. I am living my life to serve and glorify the Lord. That also means I am not living my life to gain the praise of people, including my parents. Although my Mom was very proud of me and my choice to pursue full time missions, I wasn't doing it for her. During that week I had many people tell me how I must be regretting my time away from home. How surely now I would be returning home to help care for my family. Though I had no regrets about my leaving home or serving God in this missions organization, I was now wrestling with that very question. Should I return home, what should I do now? The weight of other people's expectations now weighed heavily on me. This is something I think we can all relate to at some point in our lives.

Even without the affirmation of my Mom's co-workers sharing how proud she was of the path I had chosen, I knew that I had her full support. I knew she was proud of me. I knew she loved seeing how God was moving in my life. Fulfilling my long held dreams and answering my prayers. In fact God had blessed me with a perfectly timed goodbye phone call with her the morning of her final day with us. I was having my personal quiet time walking around the grounds of the base praying and reading the Bible when she called. It wasn't really like her to call that time of the day, and normally I wouldn't have taken a call during my quiet time. Though obviously looking back I can see God knew this was going to be our final conversation. God also knew I needed the closure that conversation would bring.

I have always loved my Mom and had a great deal of respect for her. I even aspire to be a strong woman of faith like her. However, we had our share of rocky Mother daughter experiences. Life had certainly dealt us some difficult trials and a whole lot of, brokenness. That brokenness is why I will remember our final conversation as a cherished memory.

During that conversation she specifically shared how proud she was of me. She shared how excited she was to see God fulfilling my dreams. She expressed how she hadn't always made it easy for me to leave home and that she was sorry for that. Then she shared how all she wanted for me is to live my life in full submission to the Lord. To seek Him in all things and follow wherever He leads. She cautioned me to be prayerful about all decisions and plans. To not rush ahead of the Lord, but to trust His timing. She told me to not be discouraged when other people don't understand the Lord's plans and leading in my life. That if I seek Him He will answer. And He will provide for where He is calling me. She also told me that things may not unfold the way I think they should. So don't rely on your plans so much that you stop following God's plans. She emphasized that our circumstances don't determine His calling. That I need to trust Him and follow His calling even when my circumstances change and it seems impossible. Then, she said that she knew I going to be a blessing and a source of joy for many people. She said she knew this because I was such a great blessing and joy to her. She told me that she loved me very much. I told her I love her and I will trust God's timing and follow where He leads. Then we said our goodbyes.

That final conversation ran through my head so many times that week as I wrestled over what I should do next. I felt I should return and continue to move forward with my training and plans to move to Egypt. But I was not sure what my family would think of that decision. Well, thankfully I didn't have to wait long to find out. I didn't even need to ask them. My Dad came up to me and said he knew people were telling me to come back home and help the family. But he wanted me to know that I had his full support to return. He told me he knew and Mom knew, that I was where God wanted me to be and I was fulfilling God's calling upon my life. He said I know this isn't where you belong. You are not responsible for taking care of us. As much as we will miss you, we want you to know you can go back. They wanted me to go back and fulfill my dreams, to follow where the Lord was leading me. Each of my siblings gave their support for me to return as well. So after being "home" for just one week, I said some very tearful goodbyes, and, headed back to Nashville.

Although I had peace and the support of my family to return, not everyone understood or supported my decision. Little did I know at the time that over the next two years the Lord would lead me through yet another life changing transition. In fact I was about to learn that my plans would not unfold the way I expected or hoped. Though ultimately I have discovered God's plans have far exceeded my own meager dreams and expectations.

Beauty From Ashes

Chapter four
Changing Tides
Learning To Surrender

Psalm 37:5

"Commit your way to the LORD; trust in him, and he will act."

In the midst of deep sorrow and grief I returned to Nashville. I did my best to refocus on the lectures and preparations for my upcoming move to Egypt. At the base I was surrounded by loving friends and leaders supporting my return; though not everyone thought it was wise for me to press on so quickly. Despite the concern voiced by some of my supporters, that is exactly what I needed. I needed to focus on life, hope and my future. I also needed the relational connectivity of living within the Christ centered community of the mission base. It was a place where I was daily encouraged, prayed for and wrapped in an abundance of hugs. The love, prayers and support of my missions family got me through those painful heart wrenching days and weeks that followed my Mom's passing. They helped me keep my eyes on Christ and not my sorrow, giving me hope for the days to come.

By the Grace of God I finished the lecture and prep stage of the school just before Christmas. I was well on my way to finalizing my move to Egypt, that is until I went home for Christmas break… While I was back at home on break I was made aware of many concerns the Church Missions Committee had about my moving to Egypt. Concerns that were elevated due to my decision to move forward so soon after losing my Mom. In fact they were so concerned that they were re-evaluating the financial support they were providing. They were strongly encouraging me to delay my plans and return home to my family for a while. Thankfully my family still supported my plans to move to Egypt, and as it turned out I would receive one last financial gift from my Mom.

One that not only secured that move but would provide for many other things as well.

When I came home at Christmas the family conversation turned towards my Mom's life insurance. Legally the money was left to our Dad. However, our Mom had voiced to us kids that her desire was that it be split equally among all of us. Sadly money tends to bring out the worst in people, and emotions ran high discussing this delicate issue. In the end our Dad agreed to split the money. However, he claimed that we each owed him money for various things, and he was going to take that debt out of our portion of the life insurance money. My siblings all agreed to this straight away, as they felt he may end up changing his mind if they contested this arrangement. They had all previously borrowed money from him, so they felt it was a reasonable request. I however, felt quite strongly that I did not owe him any debts. I had been working full time from the age of fourteen and had never borrowed any money from him. I politely conveyed this message to my Dad and told him he was free to keep my whole portion if he so chose. After all legally it was his. However, I also confirmed that Mom's request was for the money to be split equally among all of us. In the end my Dad decided to give me my full portion as my Mom had desired. Having this conversation and my willingness to forego the money all together was the start of healing in my relationship with my Dad.

I was no longer the hormonal teenager who felt unloved and angry with my Father. A Father who was far too often absent and neglectful of his family responsibilities. I had grown and matured beyond those painful adolescent frustrations. Even more importantly my heart had changed toward him. I had found compassion and forgiveness. Losing our Mom also brought about a change in him as well. Our Dad became more aware of how his negligence had been the cause of so much pain and brokenness within our family. For the first time in my life he began voicing his love and appreciation for us. He was also verbalizing his support and pride in my pursuit of missions and a life of ministry. He was no longer defensive of his past actions and neglect. We didn't have a lot of conversations about the past, but he finally validated his role in the brokenness of our family. I firmly believe this restoration and healing was the direct fruit of my Mom's prayers.So it was, that through her loss we gained a deeper love for one another.

With the support of my family and knowing that my finances were now in place, I had some very important decisions to make... However, before we get into that, I was recently asked how I know who to listen to in situations like this. Who's counsel do you follow when the counsel from ones spiritual authority (ie. Pastor and Missions Committee) don't align with what I felt God was speaking to me personally. As Christians we certainly have the Holy Spirit residing within us, providing discernment in the decisions we face. Yet we are also instructed to seek godly counsel and submit ourselves to those in authority over us. The Christian life is not just a personal relationship with Christ, it is a communal life within the Body of Christ, the Church. So it is important that we not cut ourselves off from the Church and the spiritual counsel within the Church. Though in this particular situation I had more than my Pastor and Missions Committee to consider. I was also under the covering of the missions organization.

Not only was I under the covering of the missions organization, but I also had my parents to consider. Although I was an adult I still felt the need, to honor, my parents and listen to their counsel in such areas. When I first began praying into pursuing missions with this organization I waited for the blessing of my parents. Even though I was an adult and free to make my own decisions, it was important that I have their blessing. It was important that I honor them, all the days of my life, as the Scripture commands us. So in this decision to move to Egypt, I had peace knowing I had my Dad's full support and had had my Mom's as well. In addition to my parents blessing, I had the full support of the leadership within the missions organization. My leaders at the missions base had come to know me quite well over the course of three schools and serving on staff. They had walked closely with me through the loss of my Mom and had great confidence of my readiness to go forward with my move to Egypt.

I had served in a variety of ministries within my home church before moving to Nashville and joining this missions organization. Yet I did not have the same depth of relationship with the Pastor or Missions Committee that I had within the leadership of the missions organization. And as I had mentioned earlier, there were some very strong differences of the Christian faith that had risen to a point requiring action. As I prayed into the timing and concerns they had voiced, I also found it important to weigh these differences. To consider the level of relationship and the root of their concerns. To examine the training I had received, as well as the level of relationship with my leaders at the missions base. And finally, where I was at in the grieving process. Though I respected the Pastor and those on the Missions Committee of my home church, I knew God had been preparing me for this move my whole life. I trusted His timing and the peace that I had in my heart that this was indeed His timing. So I began shopping for airline tickets. Appointed a power of attorney. Secured my insurance. I had an eye exam and bought two new pairs of glasses, and new luggage for my trip to Egypt. I then placed everything I would not be taking into long term storage.

I feel I should also mention in regards, to my friends question, that a large part of the decision for me was based in relationship. It came down to relationship, peace and prayer. I seriously prayed over their counsel. Both the concerns for my going so soon after my Mom's death and the general dangers of living in a muslim country as a Christian focused on missions. It is also important to note, that the friend asking was coming from a completely different dynamic of relationship. The relationship of a spiritual father. A father of confession with whom you have been in deep relationship with for many years. My relationship with the Pastor and Missions Committee was no where near as deep as that. There was a familiarity of course, but there was no depth of relationship. I knew very little of them except what I witnessed in church and the same applied to their knowledge of me. Yet, the leaders of the missions base and school I was a part of, had spent several years living in community with me. Sharing deep conversations, about my life, my faith, my dreams and aspirations for my future. We cried together through struggles and difficulties. They were aware of my weaknesses. They heard my confessions of sin. They held me accountable and encouraged me to live a redeemed life. So in many ways they were to me what the father of confession is to my friend. A source of godly counsel and authority who has a greater perspective on who you are because of the depth of relationship they have with you. That depth of relationship along with the peace I had in my heart, lead me to trust their counsel and continue my preparations.

As I had been praying about the timing and concerns that had been voiced, I felt that I should not make the transition alone. So one day while I was out at the barn with a good friend and former small group leader, I surprised her with the opportunity to travel with me to Egypt! I offered to cover all of her expenses. I asked that she pray about helping me with the initial transition and help me get an extra bag of luggage brought over. This would help keep baggage fees lower while giving me the ability to carry more familiar items to make myself at home. She was completely speechless for a few minutes. As the shock wore off she found her voice and asked how much time she had to pray about the decision. I told her I hadn't purchased a ticket yet and didn't really have a specific timeline laid out. Though I was hoping to leave in a few weeks. After recovering from the shock of my offer and praying about it, to my delight she accepted! I was thrilled to have a good friend join me for that first leg of the adventure! She also happened to be in a place of transition, so this gave her an opportunity to get away for a while to seek God for her next steps. Little did she know I bought us both one way tickets lol...

I still remember her face and slightly panicked reaction when she discovered that she did not have her return flight booked. You see we had just taken off on our overseas flight when she realized she hadn't asked about her return flight yet. I casually replied that I had bought us both one way tickets. Long pause and blank stare... I then reassured her that I would purchase her return flight whenever she felt it was time to head back to the States. But that I felt she should use this time to seek God for her next steps and lay down the worries of uncertainty. As for myself I went into this move saying, "Lord I will stay as long as You desire me to stay and I will leave whenever You should call me to leave." That declaration would certainly be put to the test as things did not unfold in Egypt quite as I had expected them too.

My second time in Egypt brought about some unexpected struggles. Struggles I wasn't sure I was capable of overcoming. I stepped off the plane with excitement, feeling encouraged and supported in this new season. But that all quickly faded into doubt and uncertainty. I was now under the leadership of people I had never met face to face. People whom I had only been in contact with for a few months. I quickly learned they had some major concerns about my being there so soon after my Mom's death. Something I wish they had mentioned before I had flown out. They were hesitant to establish any long term plans for me, and expressed that I should consider going back to the States. They were also advising I go into full time language acquisition if I did decide to stay. However, I found this approach very frustrating. I didn't want to enroll in a language school and be a full time student. I needed to feel more connected to the missions organization and have more variety in my schedule than just language learning. Thankfully my roommate was similar in this regard, which was a great blessing. She also happened to be one of my leaders within the, missions, organization. This meant I was being very closely observed in my adjustment and grieving process. Unfortunately, this was often a big source of frustration and tension. Especially since I had no real ministry involvement the first month I was there.

Because of this lack of structure the leadership there was concerned that I was staying home far too much. They thought I was possibly having culture shock and depressed in my grieving process. The truth was I was bored and frustrated and feeling lost. Not because my grief was too great or the culture overwhelming, but because I had no purpose or role. They suggested I go out to explore the city and practice my Arabic by shopping daily. For me the idea of wandering around Cairo with no specific purpose other than practicing Arabic was overwhelming and intimidating. All the fears of my childhood flooded in. I felt as though I was making myself a target for harassment if I followed their advice. Sadly sexual harassment is all too common on the streets of Egypt. This is especially true for an unveiled woman walking around alone. I have been well acquainted with this threat my whole life. Although I know how to handle myself and deflect much of it, that doesn't mean I want to subject myself to it daily. Exploring a highly populated Muslim, city alone, with shopping as a primary goal didn't interest me. Unlike most, women, I really didn't want to go shopping everyday!

I feel I should mention that though sexual harassment is all too common on the streets of Egypt, I wasn't facing it daily. It should also be known there are plenty of Egyptian men who come to your defense when others are harassing you. At least that was my observation and experience. It is also my experience that as a woman I face just as much threat from sexual harassment here in the States depending on location. This is particularly true in large cities. Yet one benefit I experienced in Egypt was the blessing of blending in to the community. This often sheltered me from the harassment. My blonde haired blue eyed roommates were not as fortunate. They dealt with far more harassment that I did. Most people just assumed I was Egyptian, so I didn't stand out in the crowd like my roommates. For that matter many still assume I am Egyptian or at least half Egyptian. Of course that lead to other struggles. Because they assumed I was Egyptian they also assumed I should know all the culturally acceptable and unacceptable behaviors and interactions. I of course did not...

As I processed my struggles with my roommate and leader, she helped me look into possible ministry opportunities. The obvious choice everyone thought of was working in a preschool. Once again I was being singled out for children's ministry. Now don't get me wrong, I obviously love children. After all I have a history of childcare and children's ministry behind me. However, that doesn't mean that doesn't mean that children are my only passion or interest. In fact when I first joined the missions organization I was hoping to explore other options. I wanted to develop other skills and areas of interest. That hadn't really panned out for me, which is why I found myself in Egypt interviewing for a position at a preschool. I spent a morning discussing my experience with children and shadowing the teachers at that preschool. That is when something inside me changed. I decided that if I really wanted to develop new skills I would have to put my foot down, so to speak. I had to force my way outside of the childcare box I found myself in. I had to find a way to show people another side of myself. I would have to step into uncharted territory and rediscover the hidden interests I had never fully developed or shared with the world.

My first step into uncharted territory came as I graciously declined the position at the preschool. Then I was faced with presenting another option to my leaders in Egypt. Not only did I need to present another option, I had to convince them that I was indeed ready to be there. I just needed to figure out how to go about that...

Given my leaders doubts about my readiness and the uncertainty of ministry opportunities, this was a difficult task. In fact I found myself questioning if I should really be in Egypt at this time in my life. Not wanting to make an emotional decision I tried my best to pray for clarity, peace and direction. I had also sought the counsel of my school leaders back in Nashville. The Lord granted me much peace in their response. They reassured me that they believed in my being fully equipped and emotionally ready for this transition. They encouraged me to continue praying and looking into the ministries the missions organization had in place. They also advised me to wait on making any big decisions about returning to the States until after my small group leader's visit a few weeks out.

As I awaited her visit, I had an amazing opportunity to attend a large gathering within the missions organization in Egypt. It was here that I learned more about each branch of ministry within the organization. Throughout the conference each branch would be sharing about their specific ministries. Talk about a very specific answer to my prayers! You see I was originally connected to a certain branch of ministry based on the school I had just completed. There were a few other things that factored in as well, but mostly it was decided by the school track.

However, this gathering gave me an opportunity to learn about many other departments and ministries I was previously unaware of. During the conference the Lord brought about several divinely appointed conversations where I was able to share what had lead me into missions. I was able to share how God had placed Egypt on my heart and how He had brought me here at this time. God also provided the opportunity to share about my recent loss and current struggles. These conversations not only gave me an opportunity to process, they also provided me with support and encouragement. They reminded me that I was not alone. I learned that others had similar experiences of losing a loved one as they were about to embark on their journey into missions. I even met others who knew the pain of losing their Mom. They extended their arms and prayers to comfort me in my grief. They also offered their support as I transitioned into overseas missions.

It was at this gathering that I was also reconnected with a familiar face from my first outreach to Egypt. I cannot even find the words to express how wonderfully comforting it was to see him across the courtyard. To know that I had a friend who truly knew me. Someone who I had spent two months with traveling all over Egypt for ministry. Truth is we weren't all that close, but he was still a familiar face. Though we hadn't gotten close during my first visit in Egypt, we connected so easily at the conference. This connection caught the eye of quite a few people who noted that I was so much more conversational with him than I was with others. In one conversation where this was brought up he described it this way. He said I am like a fortress that is sealed tight and nearly impossible to enter, but with time and the help of God I allow people to know what's inside me. I must admit that was, and may still be, a pretty accurate description.

I found everything about that gathering refreshing. It brought so much encouragement, encouragement that filled the depths of my heart. It was as though God was holding me in His arms, speaking tenderly to me of His love. He was reminding me that He was right there with me. That He would provide everything I needed and had requested of Him. It was such a sweet, sweet experience with my Heavenly Father.

I loved the times of worship and testimonies of how God was moving in each branch of ministry. It was inspiring to hear everyone share the faithfulness of God within their ministry teams and how people were coming to know Christ! It was through these sessions that I began to have a renewed hope and greater vision. I was starting to figure out where I belonged and what skills I would be developing. You see before I had left for Egypt I had decided to buy a new camera so that I could explore my interest in photography. Well, it just so happened that there was a team there where these skills could be developed and put to use. There was even a photography club I could join! My heart was filling with hope as I discovered so many possibilities and began developing friendships within other ministry teams.

I found myself connecting really well with the Revival Ministry Team. The teams focus was on encouraging the local Body of Christ through revival retreats. This team would also provide me with an opportunity to develop my photography and videography skills. They actively used both mediums throughout their service. The team provided me with a more structured schedule as they met daily for prayer, worship and retreat planning. In addition to the revival retreats they hosted, they chose to have these daily office times instead of the once a week or month meetings that some of the other teams held. This meant I would not only be going out daily, but would give purpose to those daily excursions, without the shopping! Of course I still needed to clear this transfer with the leadership team I had been assigned to when I set up my move to Egypt. This was no easy task.

Communication has never been my strength. Well, at least not a natural strength. I have had to intentionally focus on developing my communication skills over the years. Although I have worked hard on this skill, I still struggle greatly with clearly articulating myself. This is especially true when it comes to conveying my needs. In these situations I often feel burdened with guilt for having any unmet needs to voice. I become anxious and afraid by the unknown response of my audience. This anxiety was heightened because of this new place of ministry I found myself in. The unfamiliarity of the leadership paired with knowing they felt I was not ready for this move, increased my insecurity.

They not only questioned the timing of my being in Egypt, they questioned my heart and calling for the Egyptian people. The doubts they had voiced made this conversation even more difficult for me to initiate. To make things even more challenging they were now questioning my relationship with the friend from my first visit in Egypt. Because this friend was a guy, they suspected I had returned to Egypt for romantic reasons and not solely for ministry. As it turned out he was also serving on the revival team I was interested in joining, which increased their suspicions. Just to clarify, there was nothing going on relationally with him, in fact we had barely spoken to each other through emails since that first visit. I did reach out to him and another female friend when I knew I would be returning, but only because I knew of their service within the missions organization. I wanted to reconnect with them to help my transition by having a couple of familiar people to talk to.

Now because my verbal, communication skills are not the strongest, I sat down to write out everything that was weighing on my heart. Or at least a short summary of everything I was processing from my first month there. I shared this with my leaders as well as talking through my reasons for requesting the change of teams and why I felt it would be a better fit for me. After our conversation they gave their permission for me to change teams with one condition. I would continue living where I was so that they could monitor my emotional wellbeing. If they saw signs that I was struggling and needed to return to the States they would have the authority to make that call. I agreed and began making the transition into the Revival Ministry team.

It was also at this conference that my friend who had flown out with me, felt God was calling her to return home. So as promised I purchased her ticket back to Nashville and we said our goodbyes. After she left the real transition of moving overseas kicked in. Now that I was on a different ministry team I had to get up early every morning. Everyday I would head out to catch a taxi to take me to the metro train, ride the metro nearly to the end of the line and then walk to the home office where my team gathered. Did I mention I had to do that by myself? Yeah, I had to go out every morning flag a taxi and then take the metro and walk a few blocks to meet up with the rest of the Revival team. I am not easily intimidated but this experience was nerve wracking, especially the first few times. To be honest even after I felt confident in the journey, I had a few encounters that raised my anxiety.

In fact there was one time I thought I was being kidnapped by the taxi driver! It was a hot day and I was not in the mood to take the metro home so I decided to take a taxi all the way home. Now I had done this a few times so I had a general idea of the route. So when the driver agreed to the location and rate, I got in and began texting a friend. After a while I noticed we were going a different way than I had gone before, so I restated where I was wanting to go. The taxi driver said yes, yes, and repeated the location, and I said ok. However, it was taking longer than I felt it should and nothing was looking familiar. Plus the area he was driving in was not looking so safe. He then made an unexpected stop, told me to wait just a minute and went into some building. This is where I began getting very nervous.

He came back out fairly quickly and then started driving a bit further before stopping and saying okay, here you go. However, nothing was familiar to me and I told him this was not where I wanted to go. We began arguing as I insisted this was the wrong location and if he was lost he needed to ask for directions. I refused to get out of the taxi but decided to flag someone down from the street that we could ask for directions. When he asked them about the location I requested they confirmed we were not there and told him where to go. Thankfully we were soon back in familiar territory!

However, the adventure wasn't over just yet. When we stopped outside my building he demanded more money than we had agreed upon. I refused to give him more money and said it was his fault he drove to the wrong place. When he started yelling at me I stood my ground and looked him straight in the face and refused to pay more. His yelling had drawn the attention of my neighbors and he quickly drove off. I smiled and thanked the neighbors who had said something to him in Arabic that I didn't understand but had made him leave. Then I went inside and thanked God for bringing me home safely! Despite the anxiety of that taxi ride, I headed out the next morning ready to embrace my new daily routine. Egypt was feeling more and more like home.

There were many more adventures with taxi drivers during my time in Egypt. Some were not so pleasant like this one and others were really sweet nearly toothless old men that I would pay a little extra and regularly ride with because they were so kind. Riding the metro was always an interesting experience as well. Though the crowded cars were not very pleasant during peak hours or in the hottest part of the day, there are special cars just for the women. This is a great blessing when you are packed in like sardines. I remember a couple times where a man got onto the women's car by accident. The women pretty much beat the man off or into a corner of the car if the doors had closed. I felt bad for the men I saw get on board the women's cars by accident. They weren't there to harass the women they were just distracted in the rush of the crowd while boarding. But I must confess I did find it a bit funny too.

There was another funny story on the metro, where I was going somewhere with my roommates. As we are standing there talking, all these women start looking at me and this other young woman a couple people over from me. As they are bantering back and forth in Arabic I am feeling more and more uncomfortable. We could tell they were talking about me but not sure what they were saying as they were speaking quickly and a bit hushed. So my roommate decides to move closer where she quickly learns that they are trying to decide if this other woman and I, are twins or just sisters. They were all quite surprised when the learned my roommate understood them! They were even more surprised when they learned that this other young woman and myself didn't know each other and were in fact not related.

There are so many wonderful memories from my time in Egypt, it was truly a very special season of my life. Although to many it may have seemed to be the wrong timing because of the loss of my Mom. I personally found it very helpful in my grieving process. I have endured many losses in my life, and my Mom's, was by far the most difficult and sorrowful. Yet having the opportunity to be walking out in a life long dream while grieving was incredibly healing. It gave me hope and reminded me of God's faithfulness. It also forced me to live in the moment and not dwell too deeply in my sorrow. Was it also incredibly hard to be so far away from all things familiar, from everyone who knew me well? Absolutely! However, in that isolation from the familiar, God was teaching me that He is constant. He is always present and He will always meet my needs. I was learning not to put my trust, security and overall well being in the hands of people, or circumstances, but solely in God's Hands. That lesson has been reinforced many times over the years as my plans change. Relationships change. Locations change. Yet with every change God remains faithful.

My time in Egypt was full of God's faithfulness as He planted many seeds that have been brought to harvest in my life today. Through that experience God has granted me a deeper connection to my Coptic brothers and sisters. It places us on common ground and is a great conversation starter within the Egyptian community here in the States. The shared experience of life in Egypt has greatly assisted me in building relationships within the Egyptian community that I have come to know and love here in the States. I am not just some American girl curious about the culture, I am someone who truly loves Egypt and has willingly chosen to live among its people and embrace the

Egyptian culture. I was able to experience first hand the struggles they face as Christians in a country dominated by Islam. To witness the richness of their faith and the depth of their love for the Lord under Islam's oppression. Having seen with my own eyes the challenges they face, and the persecution they endure has given me a broader perspective in my journey into Orthodoxy. It is not merely something I have read about, but, it is something I have seen lived out. It is through this experience that the Lord has revealed and cultivated my faith, and brought greater understanding of the roots of my Christian faith.

Although it wasn't easy to step out in faith. To continue moving forward with my plans to return to Egypt, so soon after losing my Mom. I am so thankful that I made that choice. I am thankful that I made that choice even though I knew so many were against that decision. I am thankful because it was so difficult, and yet it was exactly what I needed in that sorrowful season of my life. I am thankful that I followed where the Lord was leading me even though it didn't always make sense. I am thankful because it was the opening of a new door. It was the preparation for a new and unexpected direction on my journey of faith. It was the beginning of bringing me where I am today.

Chapter Five
Discovering My Foundation
Finding My Faith In The Coptic Orthodox Church

Psalm 25:5

"Lead me in your truth and teach me, for you are the God of my salvation; for you I wait all the day long."

It all began with the closing of a door, and the redirection of a dream... Or at least that's how it seemed to many of my friends. Though to me it felt much more like the slamming of a door and as though someone had robbed me of my dream.

One thing I have learned in my life is that plans change. It doesn't matter how confident you are. Or how organized and well thought out your plan is. The one thing you can be certain of, is that the plan will change. Now for someone like myself, who really wants to be in control, of well, pretty much every aspect of my life. This has been a hard lesson to learn. It was especially difficult for me to accept when, once again my life was taking what seemed to me an unwanted detour. A detour that was, beyond my control. I had been so amazed by God's provision when He lead me into missions. Though it was extremely challenging and humbling to live off of the financial support of others, I finally felt as though I was living out my destiny. I know that may sound cheesy, but I really did feel as though I was finally doing what I had been created for. I also had a plan. Sure there were some aspects of the plan that were a bit fuzzy, but I had so much confidence things would work themselves out. And of course align perfectly with the vision in my head.

Then as I briefly mentioned earlier, my Mom suddenly passed away. My perfectly imperfect life began to crumble a part before my eyes. My plan to continue in full time support based missions and move overseas to my beloved Egypt slowly unraveled. Sure I had bought a one way ticket to Egypt hoping that would lead to this amazing lifetime of ministry overseas, and I was truly willing to stay as long as the Lord allowed me to stay. However, that transition was much more challenging than I anticipated. Just when I started to get over all the hurdles. Right when I started to feel confident in how things were coming together to make that plan a reality. I heard God telling me to return to the States. Why, God? Why are you taking me back to the States after only six months in Egypt? I knew He had more for me. I knew there had to be a reason why He was leading me back, though I wasn't sure what that reason was. So of course I began searching for the plan.

I thought I had discovered part of the plan, when I learned of a new school being offered in the missions organization I was a part of. The Base in Denver was starting a film school. Video production to be exact. This school would help me develop a skill I had never actively pursued, but had gained much interest in while I was in Egypt for those six months. I have always loved photography, though I had limited experience. Videography was something I always wanted to explore but never had an opportunity before my time in Egypt. So this school was an answer to my prayers. Well, at least that's what I thought at the time. Honestly, I still believe it was an answer to my prayers. I just didn't realize that God had a somewhat different plan than my own for how that would prepare for my future.

So I entered into this film school with confidence and a whole lot of vision for my future. However, by the time the school ended that vision was jumbled up with a whole lot of confusion and uncertainty. I knew the end of my time in this missions organization was coming to a close. Although I really didn't want to accept that reality, for a great number of reasons. I knew that the end was coming much sooner than I wanted, but I wasn't really ready to say goodbye. Though there were many reasons I didn't want that chapter of my life to end. The biggest reason if I am completely honest with you; is that it would leave me feeling totally out of control and uncertain about my life and future. That is another lesson I have learned in life. I have control issues, and I don't do well with uncertainty. Yet, once again I was about to enter a season of uncertainty that would stretch me and in the end thankfully strengthen my faith. Not only would it strengthen my faith and develop me in many areas, it also lead me into a season of life that often times feels unreal. Unreal in a wonderfully amazing way!

The plans I had felt so secure in, came to a heartbreaking end. Those plans came to an end full of confusion, frustration and so much uncertainty. I felt discouraged, betrayed, slandered, confused and very much alone. Of all of those, the loneliness was the worst. Now I have felt loneliness before, but there is something different about loneliness after you have lost a parent. Its this gut wrenching ache, that sadly my vocabulary is at a loss to describe, or perhaps there really are no words to describe it. So, when I finally accepted that my time was indeed coming to an end within this missions organization. That my plans were not going to even come close to unfolding, I truly felt alone. No one had the answers I needed. No one could direct me. That is no one except the Lord. The counsel of men had failed me. That counsel was split down the middle, and having had all my financial support withdrawn by the end of the year I needed some Divine intervention and fast.

I had spent my childhood feeling as though I were an adult. Yet now I found myself all grown up and feeling very much like a helpless child. I couldn't stay within the missions organization. Nor could I return to my family home and the life I had known there. All ties had been severed and the only thing I had left was God. So I did the only thing I knew to do in situations like this. I retreated from the opinions of everyone around me and devoted myself to fasting and prayer. In fact in this situation I literally retreated away from everyone. I went to stay at a friends house in another state to seek the Lord for clarity and direction. My home church, the one whom I had served in for years. The one that had just a few years earlier, sent me out fully supported and encouraged to pursue missions. Had now withdrawn their support. But that wasn't the part that hurt the most. That was just money, money that God could bring in from any source. The greater pain was from having my faith called into question. Asserting that this, missions organization, had somehow lead me astray and corrupted my doctrinal beliefs. Though they never addressed what doctrinal beliefs they felt had become corrupted. Till this day I have no idea what they felt had changed, become corrupted or out of line doctrinally speaking. What I do know is that my beliefs have not changed in any dramatic way though I have certainly grown in understanding and become much more confident in expressing them.

As I mentioned in a previous chapter, things had begun unfolding at church that had revealed long held differences between my faith and the beliefs or practices of that church. Things that as I had stated, required action on my part. Before I moved to

Nashville and began my time in missions I had known that I needed to move on from the church I had grown up in. I knew clearly that my faith didn't fully align with that denominations beliefs. I just wasn't sure where I belonged in the Body of Christ. Now there is something I should mention here. Although I grew up in two different Protestant Churches, I never became a member of a specific denomination. Though many of my Christian friends pride themselves in their denominational background and church practices. I always felt a bit saddened by the great number of denominations that exist within the covering of Christianity. I studied the history of the Protestant church both as a whole and specifically the denomination I grew up in. I also studied the Bible in school and independently and what I discovered was that things didn't always seem to line up Scripturally. I am certainly no Biblical scholar, or even a great history buff. Yet even as a child I felt there was some level of disconnect between the Scriptures and the modern day church practices or doctrine within many denominations. Yet as a child I had no ability to seek out another church. I attended church alongside my family where I continued to grow and develop in my faith and understanding of the Bible. This growth was the result of the Holy Spirit's guidance working through my desire to know God. However, I was no longer a child. It was time for me to take full responsibility for my faith. To begin that journey of defining my faith and aligning myself accordingly.

I had never felt my understanding of the Christian faith fully aligned with the church my family was attending. In fact I was quite adamant that I did not identify myself by the denomination.

I felt that too often people placed their identity and pride in their denomination instead of in Christ. This was why I would adamantly identify myself only as a Christian. This often caused friction with some of my friends and youth workers in the church. Yet, the vast array of denominations claiming to be Christian churches has always alarmed me. Mostly because it is clearly evident that they vary greatly in their beliefs concerning Biblical interpretation. For the most part I wouldn't argue over anyone being Christian, their salvation is between them and God. However, it appears that many don't have a full understanding of the history of Christianity and the church. Or only rely on sources that align with their preferred understanding. This leaves questionable gaps in doctrine and understanding that sadly can be quite destructive... Okay, enough of that, I am not sure I am qualified to go into more detail on all of this. Plus that's really not what this book is about anyway. The point I was trying to make was that I had always felt these differences of my faith from the church I had grown up in. However, I wasn't anticipating such condemnation and judgement from those I had respected as leaders in the church. Yet, through this exchange it became clear to me that it was definitely time to sever those ties. Or change my beliefs. Yet because of my convictions, I chose to sever those ties. Although, I may go into more detail on this later, for now, lets get back on track with my personal journey of faith...

Where was I? Oh, yes, I was feeling very alone and confused and in great need of God's peace and direction. So I had taken some time to remove myself from the daily grind of life. I chose to physically remove myself from everyone's counsel and opinions so I could truly hear the most important voice, God's voice.

During that personal retreat, I finally accepted that one chapter was closing and another was soon to begin. During that time away the Lord also reminded me of His great faithfulness and love. I reflected back on how He had been moving in my life over the years, through many trials and hardships. Through my reflections I could so easily see how each season strengthened me for another. That even the most painful seasons give way to great joy. I found myself full of His perfect peace in the midst of all my unanswered questions about the road ahead. I decided to focus on the practical steps I needed to take. I knew I needed to secure a job and new housing. I had a couple of viable, though temporary, options for housing so I wasn't going to stress over that. Instead I began looking into job opportunities. I started this process by going back to my strengths and experience, childcare. As I began looking into available jobs in that field in TN, I came across a website that connects families with caregivers. As I started reading bio's on families looking for Nannies I felt this could be a great option for me to secure a temporary job. At least till I could figure out long term goals that would get me back into missions. So I created a profile…

I was very detailed in my profile, and shared not only my experience as a Nanny, but shared about my faith as a Christian. I also shared my interest and experience in missions. I was utterly amazed at how quickly families began contacting me. I had only had my profile up for an hour or two when I noticed multiple families were wanting to talk with me. This was very encouraging! The website was international, so there were families all over the world seeking Nannies and Nannies seeking families. As I read through family profiles and started talking with families my excitement was growing. Then as I was browsing though the site I came upon an Egyptian family looking for a live in Nanny to care for their twin babies. I got really excited till I noticed they were located in NY... I quickly dismissed that idea. If there is one thing I know, its that I am no big city girl! Now if you know anything about Egypt, you are probably questioning how I lived in Cairo for six months if I am not a big city person. That's a fair question given the intense hustle and bustle of that big city. All I can say is God granted me the grace I needed for that season.

So knowing my preference for a smaller town lifestyle, I began talking with a family in TN who seemed very interested in my profile. As we talked it appeared that everything was lining up to join their family. Of course we all know by now that clearly what seems to be coming together according to my plans is not exactly what God ends up unfolding. So in comes God's curve ball...

Out of nowhere this family that seemed so interested stopped all communication. Then the Lord brought my profile to the attention of this Egyptian family living in NY. After reading my profile they decided they wanted to talk with me... I really wanted to say, "Sorry I am not interested," but I felt I should at least read over their profile in detail first. That's when God began changing my heart and I knew He was leading me in a direction I was not expecting. After a few detailed conversations utilizing the websites interview questionnaire it became obvious that not only did we share a heart for God, missions and a life of service. But it also seemed that we would be a great fit for each other concerning childcare needs. So we decided to take a week to pray into where God was leading in all of this.

I am sure that as you read that you already guessed that this small town country girl was about to be moving to the Big Apple! Sure enough God made it clear and gave both the family and myself peace to move forward. We began organizing the details of my move right away. It was November and I requested a few weeks to organize my things and close out my responsibilities on Base before flying out on the next leg of my adventure with God. On December, 4th 2009 I set out on a very exciting yet nerve wracking journey full of many unknowns. It was an ordinary day by all accounts, yet that one day set things in motion that would forever change my life.

One of the first things I had learned about this family is that the Dad is a Coptic Orthodox Priest. I found this very intriguing. I felt certain this was a divine opportunity I had been given to live with their family. This could be a great learning opportunity for me to grow in my understanding of the Egyptian culture and people. It would also be a huge help in preparing me for my return to Egypt. After all, before I moved out to NY, I was still hopeful that it would just be a short term position. A temporary transition that would somehow lead to my return into missions. Hopefully better preparing me for my return to my beloved Egypt. Well, it has been eight years since then. Although it was certainly a great learning opportunity, it has not brought me back to my beloved Egypt, at least not technically speaking.

My life certainly changed on December, 4th 2009, just not in any way that I was expecting. You see I was very much inclined to pursue my plan for a life of missions overseas, preferably in Egypt. That mindset made my transition out of the missions organization very challenging.

I was full of nerves as I traveled to NY that day. I was trusting God and stepping out into the great unknown, yet still trying to cling tightly to my own dream. I was excited and yet terrified of what awaited me. After all I had no idea what I was going to encounter upon my arrival. People can say what they want online or over the phone but that doesn't make it true. In this day and age you are always hearing stories of abuse and one way that traffickers capture young women is through sites like these. So I was really nervous the whole day. I know that may have been a stretch of the imagination but remember I have personally witnessed the dangers of this world growing up, so I was really nervous. I did a lot of praying that day! Thankfully, God calmed my nerves and the family was exactly what they claimed to be and so much more!

I have so many wonderfully joyous memories with their family during that chapter of my life. I mean really, twins, need I say more… Can life get any better than caring for sweet babies and experiencing the world through the eyes of a child who is seeing and discovering everything for the first time. I think not. Of course lets be real it was also full of challenges and learning opportunities for me. Experiences that I believe have brought so much growth in my life. Though I would never have thought to unfold things the way they have, God's plan has once again proven to be far better than my own!

God has taken me from a young child in Sunday school crying and pleading with Him for Pharaoh's repentance. True story, I cried and pleaded for his repentance as though it was a modern day news story. He has so intricately woven me into the Egyptian community and multiple Egyptian families as though they were my own. He has cultivated my love for the Egyptian people and granted me the desires of my heart in ways I never would have imagined. All through what I once thought was an unjust detour and the shattering of a dream. It just took me a few years before I could see His plan was so much better than my own.

I still remember a conversation the week before I flew out to NY, a friend commented on how amazing it was that God was bringing me into an Egyptian family here in the States. I wish I had been able to fully recognize then, just how amazing it truly was. That God was not providing this opportunity as a consolation prize because His original plan had been unjustly taken from me. No, this was His perfect plan unfolding in my life.

As excited as I was to be living with an Egyptian family I was still holding tightly to what I thought was the best path for my life. Clearly I was made for full time missions, preferably in Egypt. Although it took some time, I learned that God wasn't using this new door to continue in my plans. Nor was He giving me second best. He was in fact bestowing on me a far greater blessing than I could have ever imagined. He was unfolding his best for me by weaving me into the Egyptian community in ways I never could have expected.

So what was this great blessing? It was the discovery of the Coptic Orthodox Church. Not just the Church as a community or experience, it was the discovery of the Orthodox faith. Uncovering my faith within the Orthodox Church was the true blessing. It was discovering where I belong in the Body of Christ. Now this discovery wasn't quick nor was it easy. In fact it was full of frustrations, confusions, battles with my pride, tons of reading and listening and of course prayer.

I was hungry for true authentic Christianity. I was struggling and wrestling with the Lord because I felt completely severed from the church experience and background I was familiar with. I felt severed from them because the more I pursued God, the more I discovered issues of doctrine within those Christian circles. I was also upset by the secular ideology that is running rampant in many of these churches. Things that so blatantly go against the Scripture, yet are widely accepted. However, encountering Orthodoxy was honestly very overwhelming, strange and uncomfortable.

Keep in mind I am an introvert who does not like crowds of people, now throw me into a Coptic Orthodox Church in NY... It's a complete overload to my system. There is no personal space. I am being bumped and jostled and trying hard to stay close the family I have joined so I don't get lost in the crowd. However, because the Dad is a Priest, the crowds all move in closer to greet him and every member of his family. I wanted to turn around and run for my life. To step out side and breathe in some fresh air, but of course I didn't do that.

This first experience in the Coptic Orthodox Church was also my first encounter with the notoriously loud, chaotic, sticky, and distraction filled, cry room. It's been eight years since that first encounter and I still don't understand the cry room chaos. So, here I am an overwhelmed introvert, trying to set aside the crying babies and young children running wild snacking on sticky or crumbling snacks. Their Mom's eyes are a bit glazed over from exhaustion and frustration and they all seemed so defeated. Then there's me, trying to follow the apparently chaotic scene that is the Liturgy, in the midst of this madness that is the cry room.

Everything about that experience was foreign to me. It was completely overwhelming and I really couldn't get past the ineffective chaos of the cry room. As for the Liturgy, in my head I could hear all the protestant voices of my youth calling out problem after problem. Yet there was this undeniable encounter with God's presence, and in the midst of the chaos I saw His Beauty. I felt the reverence, the sanctity and the overall mystery of being in God's presence. My heart was truly captivated by Him in that encounter.

I hadn't been in NY very long before the family gave me a book to read about Orthodoxy. A book that at the time, though highly recommended by them, I really found displeasing. It was a book not only about Orthodoxy, but more specifically about becoming Orthodox. Though I read the book cover to cover and with what I felt was an open mind. It was like rough sandpaper against my pride. It felt like an attack against my entire experience of God. It challenged my faith, and a lifetime of prayerfully seeking Him and following where He leads. I was confused about why they had wanted me to read the book. Why are you trying to convert me from Christianity to Christianity? Why are you diminishing my Christian faith because I wasn't born into Orthodoxy? Why do you call me a sister in Christ with one breathe, yet speak of Orthodoxy being the one true Christian Church? A Church that I am not a part of because I unlike you were not born into Orthodoxy. Nor had I ever encountered an Orthodox Church before this point. How then can you genuinely call me, a sister, in Christ? Yet, how can anyone say I am without Christ? My entire life is covered in evidence of His presence, and my obedience to live according to His Word. It was so confusing and difficult to process. Yet I was hungrily seeking to understand and find the Truth, so despite my frustrations I pressed on.

However, I decided to forget that book, at least for the moment. Instead I decided to focus on understanding the Church and learning about the Liturgy and all these things that were so foreign to me. Thankfully I had their help and Abouna's library at my fingertips! The Liturgy was broken down for me little by little, with explanations addressing the meaning of various actions or elements. However, for someone like myself who doesn't think in terms of questions this was limited to what they felt needed explanation. To add to the confusion there were three different languages being used in the Liturgy. Plus, like in most Churches I have been to, the screen doesn't always match. So following along was a bit challenging in the beginning. I am so thankful I had some, I'll be it a small, understanding of Arabic. My love for the Egyptian people also helped with the cultural dynamics of the Church. Things that can be overwhelming and challenging for someone from a different background.

I remember during that first Liturgy being encouraged to pray along, to follow the prayers and hymns on the screen and ask questions. Now aside from the three different languages and not always being on the correct screen. I was not interested in following the prayers as much as I was interested in carefully reading them to gain understanding of the Orthodox faith. I wanted to know what they believed and make sure I agreed with the content.

I know that for someone who grew up in the Orthodox Church that may sound absurd and even arrogant. However, it wasn't coming from a place of spiritual pride as much as it was from a desire to understand. Remember I was coming from a lifetime of growing in the Christian faith. Of seeking God, reading the Bible and being devoted to live a prayerful and righteous life in accordance to His Word. I was also well aware of the sad reality that there are many churches out there that are not in line with Scripture. Although I was not 100% accepting of the protestant background I came from, I had zero knowledge of the Orthodox Church. So I was cautious. I took my time to be sure I knew what was being prayed in the Liturgy. I intently listened to the Sermons and any and all talks I was blessed to sit in on. I read books and articles and listened to teachings online, and it wasn't long before I started to attend Sunday school and the weekly Bible study.

If it hadn't been for living with Abouna's family, for his wife's encouragement and the very necessity of attending Church to help her care for the kids during the Liturgy. I probably would not have returned after that first encounter. If I had, I probably wouldn't have lasted more than a couple weeks. It saddens me to even say that. Yet in all my church experiences this was the most difficult Church community to connect with. If I hadn't come with Abouna's family, I am not even sure anyone would have reached out to me. There are many reasons for this. Just as in Egypt, I blended in fairly well. It wasn't obvious that I was not of a Coptic background. Another factor, was that it was a large Church with many new immigrants. So simply being new isn't enough to be noticed. Then of course it was also NY. A city full of busy distracted people focused on their own lives.

It was very challenging for me to build relationships. Yet building relationships was vital for me to continue in the Coptic Orthodox Church. Although fellowship and relationship with the people is not the primary reason for going to church. It is a very important part of walking out in the fullness of our faith beyond the Liturgy. We are the Church. We are the Body of Christ. We need each other. The Christian faith is not an individual, personal relationship with Christ, though certainly that is one aspect. No, Christianity is a communal faith and relationship with God and one another. We need more than to just attend Liturgy, partake of the Sacraments, and then go about our life outside the Church.

Now as difficult as it was to connect, over time I did begin building friendships. People began to see me as Ali and not just the Nanny living with Abouna's family. Even then I found the overall experience overwhelming.

Although I was discovering that my faith aligned closely with the Orthodox Church, I was greatly wrestling over the idea of becoming Orthodox. Part of this was probably my intensely stubborn nature that drives me to resist the pressure to follow the crowd. The more everyone kept saying, "You're not Orthodox YET." The more I was driven to dig my feet in and not become Orthodox. Ridiculous I know, but its true. There were other things of course, it wasn't just my stubborn pride to prove everyone wrong.

However, for me it wasn't the typical issues of a Protestant accepting the Orthodox faith either. You see I didn't have a problem or see a Biblical reason against the Icons or the intercessions of the Saints. Or anything surrounding Saint Mary for that matter. I didn't see an issue with confession or infant, baptism, or the overall patriarchal structure of the Church. Having grown up with a fairly firm Biblical foundation and being fairly well acquainted with the history of the church helped on those issues. Plus as I was now living with a Coptic Orthodox family and attending Church with them. I had a library of reading material on Orthodoxy at my fingertips and was soaking up understanding of the faith from being a part of their family.

So what was it that kept me in an internal prayerful wrestling match with God over this seemingly no brainer decision to become Orthodox? Given my love for the Egyptian people what was holding me back from this divinely appointed opportunity to become not only Orthodox, but Coptic Orthodox?

There were a couple of things that I really struggled with in my journey to become Orthodox. I will start with the easier one, community connection. On one end it was great to discover a Church where theologically and doctrinally speaking there was a unity of faith. Yet, on the other end I struggled to connect to the people. I struggled to establish relationships and fellowship within the Church. Now you may be thinking, Church isn't about social connections. You are there for God, you are there for the faith itself. If you know Orthodoxy to be true then you go and you partake of the truth and become Orthodox. I agree that sound theology and doctrine are essential to our faith, and we are not going to Church to socialize.

However, I will say it again, Christianity is a communal faith. The fellowship of Believer's, is important. We need to be in deep relationship not only with God, but with each other. Not as a way of marketing, and bringing people into the faith. But as an integral part of encouraging one another in our faith. Yet, what I experienced within the Coptic Orthodox Church was that it was very difficult to build relationships. Though most were polite, few showed interest in getting to know me. In fact I often felt invisible.

It's a very Coptic, very Egyptian, cradle Christian Church community. A community that seemed to be constantly conversing about all things wrong within the Protestant church and the dangers of its influence. So where does that leave me, someone of a Protestant background? It leaves me feeling unwelcome and anxious that I will say or do the wrong thing. That I will unintentionally convey false doctrine and lead people astray, or perhaps constantly be a source of unintentional offense. Although I have discovered that my faith very closely aligns with Orthodoxy, I obviously grew up Protestant. I inevitably will say and do things that have been influenced by that experience. This often left me feeling as though I was viewed as an enemy of Orthodoxy. That I was a danger to the spiritual wellbeing of the people. This may seem absurd to you and such a thought may have never even entered your mind. But this was a very real battle for me.

Now please hear me when I say, I really love the Coptic Orthodox Church. Sharing my battle is in no way an attack against the Church and despite the challenges; in time I did start building friendships. Friendships with amazing people whom I love dearly. I even came to a point where despite not being a big city person, I was saddened to move away from the friendships I had developed. Yet I still struggled to see myself within the Coptic Orthodox Church, because in the end I am not Egyptian. How do I fit into a community of Believer's that is so significantly defined by one nationality? A nationality that I was not born into? Even though I am often mistaken for being Egyptian and there are many who have thought I grew up in the Church, I still felt like an outsider. So what made me stay? It was my love for the Orthodox faith and the Egyptian people that prevented me from giving into my emotions. It was love that kept me from walking away from the challenge of connection. Although it was and even to some degree still is a battle for me to connect and build relationships within this community. Love keeps me rooted.

Another facet of my struggle for relationship comes from my educational background and career pursuits. More specifically, the fact that I haven't pursued educational degrees, titles or a socially prominent career. Now to be fair, this has set me a part generally speaking within every social circle I have been a part of since I graduated high school, at least to some extent. However, my choice in this, is by far, much more absurd and unheard of within the Egyptian community. Therefore it has caused many to pull back or try to challenge me to rethink that choice. In fact, I can often see them cringe and almost panic when they learn that I don't have a college degree. Once they learn I am working as a Nanny, I have usually lost them completely.

You see in the Egyptian community you are a Dr., Lawyer, Engineer, Dentist, or some other highly educated professional. So it's not surprising they are so taken aback by my career choice. Now of course not everyone pulls away when they learn my profession. For those who have taken the time to get to know me, I am well loved and respected. I am known for being intelligent, creative, having a wide array of knowledge and experience. Someone who is highly skilled, talented and sought out as a Nanny. I am highly sought out because I bring far more than just basic childcare to the families in which I serve. That is all just professionally speaking. Yet, for many just hearing that I am a Nanny dismisses me from any further interest of relationship. It's as though ones career choice defines ones character and relational qualities.

It is painful to know that some people think less of you simply because your education level or career choice doesn't meet with their standards. This is especially true when you would never accept or reject someone based on such things. Yet it has happened repeatedly when people hear I am a Nanny. Countless conversations have ended at the mention of my career choice. But what baffles me most about this is that it implies the only thing I have to offer is my childcare abilities. That all anyone has to offer is directly linked to their career, and nothing more. Obviously that is ridiculous, and I doubt anyone would actually say such a thing. Yet when the only thing you are interested in knowing about someone is their education level and career status, what else is to be concluded?

I know that my career choice is hardly glamorous nor is it highly profitable financially speaking. It is in no way prestigious, nor will it secure for me a cushy retirement. Yet I cannot think of another job that I would love nearly as much. Nor could any salary, title or honor given by an institution compare with the honor, love and sincere gratitude that is bestowed upon me by the precious families with which I have been blessed to serve. What greater honor is there than to be entrusted with the precious life of someones child. To care for them, protect them and be one of the first people to teach them as they discover the world around them. What greater love, besides that of Christ Himself, is there than the love of a child full of innocence and free of judgement or conditions. In addition to the pure unconditional love of a child I am blessed by the deep love and gratitude of their parents and extended family members. A love that continues to grow deeper when they experience the peace of God knowing that their children are being well cared for and loved while they are away.

You see for me it's not about securing a financially sound future. Being a Nanny is not simply a job or career choice. It's about following my passion and utilizing my God given abilities and talents. I was never career minded. It was always my desire to live a life of service. Through pursuing a life of service the Lord has blessed me far beyond my plans. He has woven me into the Egyptian community that captured my heart as a child. He has granted me the blessing of serving and becoming a member of many families by working as a Nanny. Within this circle of families I have been blessed to serve, I am well loved and highly spoken of.

As loved as I am by the families in which I have served, I needed relationships within the Church that extended beyond these families. I needed relationships that went beyond my career. Now I feel I should mention that I had developed some wonderful friendships that went beyond those families. However, the pace of NY life limited the growth of those friendships. That is where my move out of NY came into play.

Let's talk about NY. I spent five years living in NY, five years living within the Egyptian community there. I was a part of two different Egyptian families where I found myself wrestling over becoming Orthodox. Those five years were amazing. Though at the same time extremely challenging. I went into that first Nanny position thinking it would be a fairly short term experience. One that would hopefully give me greater understanding of the Egyptian culture and possibly open up some doors. Doors that would provide me with some connections that would help me return to missions in Egypt. Then of course I began discovering Orthodoxy. Things were not unfolding the way I had first imagined they would. For the first time in my life I could almost feel roots beginning to form. That first job turned into a much longer commitment than originally expected. That transitioned into a second Nanny position, which of course was in the same Coptic community, albeit a different Church. Life certainly wasn't unfolding the way I thought it would. Although I had begun building some really wonderful friendships within the Church community, I was growing weary of the NY lifestyle. I was worn out by the constant busyness and long hours that are required in such a career oriented environment. I was worn out in my wrestling match with God over my future within Orthodoxy.

I had not even been with the second family for a year, when I found myself feeling completely depleted. I knew I needed a change. I knew that change meant leaving NY and establishing a more balanced lifestyle. Yet I felt so selfish making that decision. I loved this family and I knew this family depended on me for childcare. However, I knew I had to make a change and begin taking care of myself as much as I take care of everyone else. After months of agonizing prayer, I made the heart wrenching decision to leave. I gave my notice to the family and began praying for an open door. At this point I had finally come close to making the decision to become Orthodox. In fact I knew that was what God was asking of me. Despite knowing this was where God was leading me, I chose to lay that decision aside. I was so exhausted and overwhelmed with all that was going on. I felt so broken and confused with my life. I also felt as though I had completely failed this family I had been working for. I knew I needed to leave NY but I didn't know where I was going and I didn't even want to think about finding another Orthodox Church.

Chapter six
Becoming Rooted
Choosing Orthodoxy

Colossians 2:6-7

"As you therefore have received Christ Jesus the Lord, so walk in Him, rooted and built up in Him and established in the faith, as you have been taught, abounding in it with thanksgiving."

So how then did I come to finally choose Orthodoxy? What greater struggle made me hesitant to fully embrace the Coptic Orthodox Church that had in so many ways deeply captivated my heart? We have established that it had been eight years since I was first introduced to Orthodoxy and more specifically the Coptic Orthodox Church. Yet it wasn't a full eight years that I wrestled with choosing Orthodoxy. Although I had come to a place of closure with the church I had grown up in by the time I moved out to NY. I wasn't really sure where I could find a church that had the doctrinal foundation I was looking for. It was a very scary place in my journey. I knew I needed the spiritual nourishment and connection of being a part of the Body of Christ. Yet, I had come to a place of dissatisfaction with the American church experience. There were too many issues of doctrine and teachings that I found in conflict with the Bible. I struggled with the casual entertaining environment that had become "church".

Then I found myself living with a Coptic Orthodox family. Not just any Coptic Orthodox family, it was a Priest's family. I found myself attending church with their family as a part of my job. After all you remember my description of the cry room, and the fact that they had twins. They definitely needed my help! I also needed to be in church for my own spiritual growth and nourishment. That was how things began. Yet, I was also curious to learn more about the Coptic Orthodox Church. Even if at first my curiosity was mostly because of my love for all things Egyptian. Though my curiosity for wanting to learn more about the Church was not wholly spiritual, God quickly captivated my heart at a spiritual level. That first chaotic encounter with the Liturgy revealed to me not only the presence of God, but the depth of reverent worship that I had been longing for.

During that first Liturgy God awakened something in me that filled me with a hunger to know more. In that moment He truly captivated my heart with the desire to seek greater understanding of the roots of my Christian faith. It didn't take long for me to discover that Orthodoxy is the best preserved Christian Church. Yet despite recognizing it to be the original and purist Christian Church, and even seeing how well my own faith aligned with the Orthodox faith. I struggled to truly and fully embrace Orthodoxy.

Setting aside the challenges of building relationships within the Church that I had mentioned earlier. The greater battle in accepting Orthodoxy, was how to reconcile my identity as a Christian outside of Orthodoxy, not only my own identity as a Christian. But that of family, friends and even perfect strangers, coming from a Protestant Evangelical background. After all, I had spent my entire life devoted to the Lord. My whole identity was in Christ and my faith was sincere, and rooted in the Word of God. My life was full of the evidence of God's presence and the work of the Holy Spirit. Yet it would appear that from an Orthodox perspective I couldn't truly be a Christian?

How do I reconcile my entire lifetime living and identifying my self as a Christian? What is my identity if not in Christ, and not just my own identity in Christ but countless friends, family and all those outside the Orthodox Church? It was an even greater struggle for me because the more I read about the Orthodox faith, the more I saw my own faith. Yet I still found myself outside of Orthodoxy because I hadn't been born into it, nor had I ever encountered an Orthodox Church before. So obviously I had never been baptized into the Orthodox faith. The issue of baptism and communion was a great part of my struggle. Because although my beliefs lined up concerning both, as far as, I agree they are essential for our salvation, and they are sacramental. A mystery of God not just a symbolic practices many Protestant believe. Yet, simply sharing this belief didn't change the reality that I grew up in Churches that are not aligned within the apostolic tradition. (not sure about the phrasing)

Even though I have since been, baptized into the Coptic Orthodox Church. A decision that has taken, what eight years for me to come to. I am not sure I have a sufficient answer concerning Protestant Christians. I certainly can't deny the Lord's presence or the work of the Holy Spirit in my life. Yet, I also believe Orthodox Christianity is the original Christian Church and the Sacraments found within Orthodoxy are essential to true Christianity. However, they are not Sacramentally found within Protestant Churches. I have wrestled over this for years, even before discovering Orthodoxy. I didn't understand or agree with the Protestant view of symbolism only.

 Yet when so many of you, my Coptic Orthodox friends, have asked why I struggled with deciding to truly become Orthodox. When it was so clearly evident that my faith is Orthodox and my heart for the Egyptian people is so widely known. Try for just a moment to place yourself in my shoes. I like you grew up within the doors of a church. I have grown up reading the Bible and praying to the God of the Bible, the God of Abraham, Isaac and Jacob. I like you was baptized and grew up partaking of communion. Believing fully that baptism and communion is more than just a symbolic practice. Believing that in Baptism we die with Christ and are then raised to new life with Christ. Believing that the bread and wine of communion is truly and mysteriously the life giving Body and Blood of Christ. Then one day as an adult I encounter Orthodoxy, and my baptism is not recognized as anything but a symbolic act. My whole identity as a Christian is considered to be nothing more than an introductory course along the pathway, to Christianity. It is not considered the real thing. Would you so easily and quickly accept that answer and join yourself to this Church?

Truly, my journey into Orthodoxy has been long, probably much longer than most. Many of you have encouraged me along the way and yet wondered why it took me so long to make the decision to become Orthodox. I don't know if its possible for someone who grew up in the Orthodox Church to fully understand that struggle. To recognize the process and journey I have been on, in coming to Orthodoxy. I have hungrily sought out truth, pursued deeper understanding, and devoted myself in prayer. I have fought physical, mental, emotional, relational and spiritual exhaustion on this journey of faith. Pride and fear were my two strongest opponents. They repeatedly beat me down, paralyzing me from making a decision one way or the other. Although it has been a long journey, I have been so encouraged by God's mercy and love along the way. I have also been deeply blessed by the love of my friends who have stood with me and supported me, allowing me to take my time in the process.

I wish I could say that in this long process I have fully overcome my pride and fear. That I have discovered all the answers and understanding possible for our human mind to comprehend. But of course I haven't. However, I have grown in many ways and though I certainly don't have all the answers or understanding. I have found peace with not knowing everything I desire to know and understand. I have also come a long way in slaying my pride and fear, though I know that will be a life long battle. Because of my limited ability to understand the depth and mystery of God, a depth and mystery that simply goes beyond our human comprehension. I must accept that there are some things I won't have answers to. What I can tell you is that I have read extensively and will continue to do so. I will seek to know and understand in greater detail and I will do my best to walk in obedience to the knowledge and understanding of truth that God gives me. This is why in the end I have chosen Orthodoxy.

As I mentioned in the previous chapter, there was a point in time, while I was still living in NY, where I first came to a place of decision. In that season I knew that I needed to choose Orthodoxy. I knew that was what God was asking of me. I knew that it was the right path to grow closer to God. To continue on the road of my salvation and redemption. I remember even writing a blog sharing the news that I knew I could no longer court the Church. That just as in a courtship there comes a point where you need to move forward into marriage or you need to walk away; and I had reached that point. Yet, just as I started this book out speaking of the reality of spiritual warfare. I was once again thrown into a spiritual battle when I came to that awareness and decision. Life began to get bumpy. Once again I found myself facing an unexpected transition and the uncertainty of my future. You would think I would have been used to that kind of thing by now. But I must admit I didn't handle that change very well. I became overwhelmed and distracted by the chaos of this new transition and the emotional rollercoaster that accompanied those changes. My life was thrown completely off balance. I became just as chaotic internally as the streets of NY are externally. Simply put, I was a mess.

So what was this transition that threw me so off balance? The time had come to move on from the wonderful Coptic Orthodox Priest's family. A family that had become my own, a family I will always be a part of and a family I deeply love. It was not the smoothest of transitions. Although it was clear the time had come for us to part ways, it wasn't easy to say goodbye, it never is. I had been with them for so many joyous celebrations and through some of life's most difficult hardships. They had embraced me as their own family even granting me the blessing of adopting my sweet puppy Jericho. Oh, the stories I could tell of that experience. Lets just say puppies are not for everyone and Jericho is by far the most needy and challenging pup I have known. However, I am forever grateful that they gave me the blessing of taking him on as my own. Now this part of the story has yet another curve ball, where once again I experience God's perfect timing and provision. You see Jericho was fathered by a dog I had left with my parents when I was in full time missions. After my

Mom passed away, my Dad inherited Kenobi, Jericho's father, eventually finding himself with a house full of puppies. Anyway, I ended up being given the opportunity to bring one home to NY all the way from IN where my Dad was living. Now here is where God really provides in such intricate and personal ways...

As I have shared before, I never really had a good relationship with my Dad. Although it certainly improved after losing my Mom, my Dad's offer of Jericho was tangible evidence of God's redemption in our relationship. This was the first time in my entire life that my Dad gave me a gift. The very first time he had ever given me a gift. Not only was it the first gift he had ever given me. It was a very thoughtful gift, a gift backed by his love and knowledge of me. I don't think I will ever be able to find the right words to express my gratitude to Abouna's family for giving me the opportunity to adopt Jericho. To receive such a thoughtful gift from my Dad was a blessing beyond words. As amazing as that was, the depth of the gift and their generosity to allow me such an opportunity cannot be fully understood without a few more details.

I picked Jericho out from this wild collection of puppies my Dad had inherited while on a visit to my family. That alone made the visit much more enjoyable. Visiting my family since moving away has always been an emotionally difficult experience for me and this was no exception. Though I had originally planed on flying back to NY, adopting Jericho changed those plans. Instead I was faced with a long drive from IN to NY, just me, my Dad and Jericho. I must admit I was not entirely excited about that drive. Yet during that long drive God brought full healing and closure in my relationship with my Dad. Closure I would only a month later tearfully be thanking God for. You see that trip was my very last experience with my Dad, and though I didn't know it at the time it was our very last goodbye. A month later I would get another heartbreaking phone call from my sister letting me know that he had passed away.

Once again I was grieving the loss of a parent. I was broken and despite being an independent adult I felt very much like an orphaned child. Suddenly it felt as though I was alone in the world. My sister's had there families, and my brother had my sister's but I was living across the country with no family near by. Although I had always felt pretty content in my singleness, losing both parents made my singleness feel even more lonely. However, God had so perfectly provided me with the most loving companion to help me through my grief, my sweet puppy Jericho. Believe it or not I don't place him above my wonderful human friends and family, though I know a few have wondered about that. God has certainly blessed me with amazing human friends, friends who came alongside me during that season of sorrow. Yet, there is just something about a dogs ability to sense your emotional needs without you needing to say a word. It is a truly amazing fact. One that has repeatedly done wonders for my heart.

So you see Jericho was not only a thoughtful gift from my earthly father. He was a gift given in perfect timing by my Heavenly Father as well. He has brought so much joy to my heart and driven me crazy with his excessive shedding and socially challenging fears of being separated from me. Yet I love him and treasure him because he is the first and only gift from my Dad.

Although Jericho is just a dog he holds a very special place in my heart and has comforted me so many times over the years. However, as I faced the transition away from my first Orthodox family, Jericho was not only a source of comfort he was also a challenging obstacle.

Once again I found myself needing to figure out what comes next. Only this time I was far more stressed than excited about that process. This time, I had Jericho to consider, as well as myself. Although I don't consider him to be my child as some pet parents do, in this situation I really did feel like he was my child. I couldn't even think about having to give him up. Yet finding large dog friendly housing, in NY, that would fit within the budget and schedule of a Nanny is difficult. Thankfully God really does work in mysterious ways and always provides for our needs in His perfect timing. At just the right time God provided yet another wonderful Coptic Orthodox family for me to Nanny for, and they amazingly enough welcomed Jericho as well! God really is a loving Father who delights in His children and takes our concerns and interests to heart. Nothing is too small and trivial to take before our Heavenly Father.

Although God had once again provided for my needs, it was still a difficult transition and adjustment for me to make. Internally I was a mess. Trying to process all my emotions with the transition, the logistics of a new location and job. It wasn't long before I physically began feeling the imbalance of my years living in NY. I am a country girl at heart so the constant busy lifestyle of NY, paired with the realities of working as a live-in Nanny had really begun wearing me down. I loved this new family, as I really love each family God has placed me with over the years. But I felt as though I wasn't able to give them my best because I was feeling so worn out. I wasn't up to fulfilling the requirements of the position to the standard of excellence that I place upon myself. This added greatly to my emotional battle. I found myself battling with that all too familiar desire for perfection. Yet, physically, emotionally, relationally and most importantly spiritually I found myself depleted.

I spent a year wrestling with all of this. Praying and arguing the counsel of good friends who advised I walk away because they saw how worn out I was. Yet I couldn't let myself fail this family by walking away from a position to soon. I was also uncertain of where would I be going… Ultimately, I stayed for that year because I didn't feel peace to leave. Though at the same time I felt myself becoming dangerously off balance and weak. I had completely tossed aside my decision concerning Orthodoxy. All my energy was focused on my job and just surviving daily life. As that year passed by I came to a breaking point where I knew I needed to make a change or my physical health would soon be affected. I knew it was time to start focusing on caring for myself as much as I care for others. That meant having to walk away from a family I loved and who loved and depended on me. It was an incredibly difficult decision for me to make and I felt so horrible having to give my notice. But I knew I needed to move away from NY and step away from being a live-in Nanny, at least for a time.

Despite giving my notice, I was committed to honor my original commitment. Although we didn't have a contracted commitment concerning how long I would work for them. I had committed to giving them plenty of time to make other arrangements concerning childcare before leaving. I always like to give the families I work for several months notice when the time comes. After all lining up childcare is one of the most important things for a parent to arrange. They need to have peace and confidence about their childcare. So now I had about four months to help them line something up as well as figure out where I would be moving and what kind of work I would be doing.

Once again I found myself on the verge of the unknown. Yet, this time I was confident about making the transition. I was even hopeful that perhaps I would be returning to missions. I contacted a few close friends asking for their prayers and explaining my desire to move back down south. I shared that I was very seriously thinking about leaving behind my days as a Nanny and instead returning to missions. Within about 24-48 hours of sharing this news and prayer request, I was contacted with a phone call that would forever change my life. A change that would once again leave me in awe of God's great love for me. He was preparing a whole new chapter, one that has been so full of blessings, Love, and one that fills my heart with deep gratitude daily...

It always amazes me how perfectly the Lord provides. How lovingly He works in our lives to bless us. Even when we struggle to trust Him or we wrestle to make our own plans work instead of fully surrendering them to Him. God faithfully provides for our every need. Although I had chosen to lay aside my decision to become Orthodox, having given into my utter exhaustion, the

Lord would not leave me wandering in uncertainty. Instead He planted me by streams of living water, where I could find rest and refreshment. He opened a door for me that was completely unexpected. One that has continued to amaze me daily, by the abundance of His intricate love for me. Not only does He leave me amazed by His love for me, but I am continuously amazed by the love of others for me as well. I have truly been adopted into this current family that I am working for. Although that could be said of the previous families as well, there is just something unexplainably different that sets this "adoption" apart. My relationship with this family really is familial. They are my family, my sister's, brother's, parents, grandparents, nieces and nephews. They welcomed me in at my lowest and most broken, yet have fully recognized and encouraged me in my strengths. They actively seek to know and meet my needs. There is just a very special bond, that runs deep with each member of the family. A bond that surpasses the working aspect of my being a Nanny.

Another thing that really set this current position apart from the others was that initially I only had one child in my care. I honestly can't recall ever having just one child in my care, so that was a whole new and refreshing experience for me. Yet God knew exactly what I needed in terms of restoration from the hectic pace of life I had experienced in NY. He provided perfectly for that restoration through my move to Houston. Although I knew that I was in need of rest and balance, it wasn't until I had made the move and been working for a few months that the reality of my exhaustion hit. Despite that realization it was still a struggle for me to focus on rest and healing. The battle to always be accomplishing something, contributing and serving others was difficult to overcome. I made the move with unrealistic expectations for myself to quickly achieve my goals of health, balanced work life, expanding my social life, and plugging into the local Church. So when I discovered that my health wasn't improving quickly, because I was utterly exhausted. Or when I felt completely out of place at Church and building a social life was more than I could handle. I felt defeated and discouraged.

I felt as though I was never doing enough. Yet I had no strength or energy to do more. I found myself wallowing in self condemnation, tearfully pleading with the Lord to help me. The thing is, I wasn't prepared for His response to my pleas. The more I cried out for strength and energy, or connection and relationship. The more I heard Him lovingly speak to me to just be still. To rest, to stop striving and trying to make everything happen, and just rest. At work I felt like I wasn't doing enough. It was way too easy. Yet they continuously showed their appreciation and love for me. They weren't adding on responsibilities, and in fact they were always sensitive to keep my work load light and as stress free as possible.

 God had brought me into a season of life where He wanted me to truly grasp the depth of His love. He wanted me to know that it isn't something that can be earned. It isn't based on what we can do for Him or for others. Of course I knew this in my head, but I discovered that I was still greatly struggling with that need to be perfect. To be strong and provide for others so that I would be worthy of love. So now I found myself having to learn how to accept love when I didn't feel worthy of it because all I could see was my weakness.

It's been nearly four years since I moved down here and I am still working on learning this. It's still challenging for me to embrace all their love without feeling like I need to be doing more to deserve it. It has been a very surreal three and half years for me. I am growing healthier and stronger. I have established some incredible friendships and of course the biggest change has been that I have finally become Orthodox. My life may not look exactly as I imagined when I first set out on my journey with God all those years ago. Yet He has once again amazed me with how much greater His plans are than any plans we could create on our own. He has also shown Himself faithful to answer my prayers and grant me the desires of my heart as I truly delight myself in Him. As I seek Him in every season of my life He is faithful to reveal more of His great love for me. He is faithful to lead me through the uncertainties into the beauty that awaits as His plans unfold.

Chapter Seven
Abundant Life
Embracing The Fullness Of God's Love

1 Chronicles 4:10

"And Jabez called on the God of Israel saying, "Oh, that You would bless me indeed, and enlarge my territory, that Your hand would be with me, and that You would keep me from evil, that I may not cause pain!" So God granted him what he requested."

Many years ago, or at least sometime shortly after high school, the college Sunday school class spent a few weeks on the prayer of Jabez, found in 1 Chronicles. I remember really being drawn to his short simple prayer. It was a prayer that truly resonated with my heart. I wanted those very same things, for the Lord to bless me and enlarge my territory, for His hand to be with me and for Him to keep me from evil, that I may not cause pain. I wanted my life to be a blessing to others because God was with me. I wanted His blessings so that I could be a blessing and I desperately wanted to expand my territory and move beyond the city I had always known. Well, fast forward a few years and it is abundantly clear, God has truly granted me what I requested, just as He did for Jabez.

After coming to the realization that I needed to leave NY to start taking better care of myself, my mind came back to this prayer. I knew I needed to care for myself so I could truly be a blessing to others for many years to come. However, I also knew that God had to be the one to lead me into the next chapter of my life. When I sent out the news of my leaving NY I shared that I was praying into a possible return to missions. I felt hopeful that God would once again grant me that request and perhaps this time He would lead me into missions long term. I still had in mind this life of missions overseas. I honestly struggled with feeling as though working as a Nanny was not really living a life of service. I know its crazy, because clearly working as a Nanny is a great service to the families I work for. However, at the time I wasn't really seeing the bigger picture of what I do as a Nanny. My time in missions had left me feeling that this was just like any other job. So when I received a phone call from a total stranger, offering me a chance to continue working as a Nanny... I was a bit perplexed.

What is God doing? Yet, the timing and the connection was unmistakably divine. So, although I personally did not know the family offering me this job opportunity I was surprisingly open to the possibility. Though I didn't know them, a very good friend of mine knew them well. In fact just a day or two earlier I had sent this prayer request to that friend which lead to this unexpected phone call. Oh, and it was yet another Coptic Orthodox family! Hmm, yeah I would call that a total God connection!

It was a very humbling experience for me to find myself so weak and utterly depleted, yet still chosen, loved and greatly appreciated. There is not a day that has gone by in these past few years that I have not felt loved and incredibly blessed. In fact I often feel overwhelmed and undeserving, of the great love and favor that I have experienced here. Just another one of my life long struggles being worked out. The struggle to believe I am loved, desired and appreciated just as I am. It is that feeling of never being enough, and striving to be perfect in everything, yet always so aware of my flaws and weaknesses. This struggle like many others is rooted in my childhood.

The transition out of NY and into my new home in Houston Texas, was much more difficult than I had anticipated. I quickly learned just how worn out I had truly become. I came down full of excitement and ambition to restructure my life and finally experience balance. Some of my biggest goals were to build friendships and plug into the local Coptic Orthodox Church. After all I hadn't forgotten that place of decision I had come to back in NY. The one where I knew God was calling me to fully commit myself to the Orthodox Faith. However, things did not go quite as I expected. The reality of my exhaustion and brokenness hit hard once I was in a place where things had balanced out and slowed down.

It wasn't long after arriving in Houston that I learned that finding balance and taking care of myself was going to be much more complex. It was more than just a change of location and different working hours. Though that was certainly a refreshing change I was far more exhausted than I had realized. Just getting out of bed on the weekends was difficult. I had also quickly discovered that it was just as challenging to connect to the Coptic Orthodox Church here as it had been initially in NY. This was definitely discouraging. After struggling for a couple months I finally realized I needed to stop striving. I needed to trust the message I felt God had spoken, to be still and rest in Him. I decided to stop striving for everything and instead invest in my physical needs first. I chose to focus on rest and recovery. I allowed myself to sleep as much as I needed to on the weekends even if it meant I wasn't making it out to Church. This was so difficult for me. I felt guilty, yet I knew that my physical health had declined to a point where it was necessary to prioritize rest above Church.

I also had to make some significant dietary changes. My eczema had gotten horribly out of control and the lower stress of my new position hadn't corrected the outbreaks. So I began researching causes which ultimately lead me to an elimination diet. It was a bittersweet experience when I learned that gluten was a strong contributor my eczema. Going gluten free was and still is a huge challenge for me. Though it has also been a great opportunity for me to expand my skills in the kitchen! My extreme fatigue and eczema were not the only health related issues I was facing. I found myself in the most excruciating pain one day while I was at work. Now I am not one for going to Dr.'s in fact I have anxiety about going to the Dr. because of several horrible experiences with Dr.'s. So when I found myself asking to be taken to the Dr. I knew there was something seriously wrong. As it turned out I had a kidney stone. This lead to several hours in the emergency room getting rehydrated and managing the pain. This is also when I came to the horrifying reality of my weight gain. My health was so out of control and I was so discouraged by all these struggles. Although I have been overweight for much of my life, it hadn't ever slowed me down or kept me from living an active life. But in that moment I knew something change.

Though that realization initially sent me into a bit of an emotional tailspin, I soon reminded myself that God is with me. He brought me into this season so that I can be renewed and refreshed. I refused to give in to the self depreciating thoughts from my past that caused me to struggle with my self worth. It didn't matter that I didn't live up to the worlds standard of beauty, or even my own unrealistic expectations of perfection. I made a decision in that moment to dismiss the voices I had battled with for years. The statements people had made directly or whispered thinking I couldn't hear. The rejection and criticism from guys who couldn't see past my physical imperfections. Even my own harsh judgements and comparisons. Though those memories and thoughts tried to rush into my mind repeatedly, I chose to focus on truth. The truth that God had brought me into a season where He was truly transforming my mind and healing the brokenness of my past. The truth that my identity and worth are in Christ. Part of that healing came through the people He had surrounded me with. People who were daily encouraging me, loving me and embracing me as I am. Something inside me was shifting and for the first time in my life I was filled with confidence and contentment. I was learning to see myself not through the lens of all my flaws and brokenness but through the lens of God's work within me. I was recognizing all the ways God has moved in my life. How He has developed so many skills, talents and passions through the struggles I have endured.

You see when I had first gotten that call about this Nanny position in Houston, I was very transparent about my state of exhaustion. I had clearly shared my need for a healthier more balanced life, including my work load. Yet they still chose me. Although I was still seeing myself through my weaknesses, they were seeing me through the eyes of those who knew me. Through the eyes of my friends and the Priest's family whom I had worked for. Who had shared with them all the ways I had used my strengths to be a blessing in their lives and families. And now nearly four years into this job, I am finally seeing what they have all seen. I am seeing my strengths, and beauty. I am seeing both my inner and outer beauty. I am finally seeing the many ways the Lord has blessed me, so that I too am a blessing in the lives of those around me. I am seeing that He has granted me that life of service that I have sought Him for. Even though it is not overseas doing "missions" work, it is truly a ministry to the families He has placed me within.

So as I began to see my life through this new perspective, I began to find physical and emotional healing. At that point I decided to direct my prayers to my relational and spiritual needs. Now when you are in your 30's and still single yet, pretty much everyone you know is married with kids, it can be quite challenging to develop your social life. However, this is my reality. So although my frustrations with connecting to people within the Church, hadn't really changed, God certainly wasn't phased by that obstacle. He has been faithful to meet my relational needs in ways I never expected. The first place He has done that is within the family I am working for. God has established not just employment with them, but friendship and family as well.

Then in perfect God timing He also brought about a new Coptic Orthodox Church. A mission Church whose focus is on bringing Orthodoxy, to those like myself, who do not come from an Orthodox background! This was so unexpected, yet came as I had finally learned to rest in Him and stopped striving in my own strength. One of the great blessings that came from this new Church was the friendships. It was such a different experience encountering a Coptic Orthodox community that was instantly engaging me.

So my journey into Orthodoxy, got a fresh start in October 2016 with a simple invitation. An invitation to go to Church with one of my new friends and her husband. At the time I was still a bit hesitant and not sure what to expect. Yet that first car ride to Church was filled with wonderful conversation that left me feeling so encouraged. When we arrived I found myself warmly greeted by so many people just upon entering the Church. It felt wonderful to be back in Church! And just like my very first experience with the Liturgy I found it to be so refreshing and life giving. It felt like coming home. I knew in my heart this is where I belonged, but I still wasn't ready to commit. Though I knew in my heart that Orthodoxy is the original, purest Christian faith. I was still wrestling with my Evangelical background and the wide circle of Evangelical friends whom I love and respect. What would it mean for those relationships if I became orthodox? How would they change and would I end up being cut off from some of my closest friends if I made such a life changing decision? There was one particular relationship that was at the forefront of my mind. You see I had just started a long distance online relationship with a guy, who although he was Egyptian, was not Orthodox. He was Evangelical…

It was exciting to finally have someone actively pursuing me. Someone who was involved in full time missions with the same missions organization I had been a part of just over 8 years ago. On the surface there appeared to be many things supporting the relationship and our compatibility. Yet the more I prayed into the relationship the more I knew it wasn't what God wanted for me. I began seeing red flags all over the place. All the compliments and praise began to feel insincere and rooted in insecurity. We weren't getting to know each other very well because he was far too agreeable. Our conversations never went deeper than compliments and surface level statements of agreement. This was despite my actively trying to go deeper. Yet I was still trying to remain hopeful, to be more vulnerable than what I naturally tend to be. I know I can be very guarded so I was trying to step out of my comfort zone and really give the relationship a chance.

As I was prayerfully pursuing this relationship, I had sought the prayers of a few close friends as well as reading through a few Christian relationship books. Now I have always covered my desire for a husband in prayer. In fact I have been praying for my future husband since I was a child. Although I was feeling a bit of uncertainty about this guy, I didn't want to retreat too quickly. I felt God was using this relationship to stretch me beyond my comfort zone. Especially in the area of communication and confrontation, the two areas I have always been quick to just walk away from when things don't go smoothly. So although I eventually ended things with him, I still feel that it was a fruitful experience for me. In fact, in many ways it was the catalyst towards my becoming Orthodox...

You see I was face to face with a very real possibility of marriage. A desire I have held in my heart my whole life. He was a Christian. He was Egyptian. He was living a life of service and ministry. He loved children, animals and nature. He ticked off so many boxes of things I have prayed for in a husband. It was as though God was handing me this perfect answer to years of prayer. However, there was a catch. In order to have that dream fulfilled I would have to deny the conviction in my heart that Orthodoxy is the wholeness of my Christian faith. I would have to choose marriage over Orthodoxy.

I felt as though God was saying, "Ok, Ali, where is your heart? Is your heart truly with Me? Are you truly committed to seeking Me first? Do you really want to be rooted deep in Me, or are you content to live in the shallows of your faith?" This relationship was mine for the choosing. But was I willing to pay such a high price? Now, for those of you who heard me share some of the red flags and frustrations of this relationship, you are probably thinking of course it was not meant to be. It probably seemed to be an easy decision to end things. Yet this was not an easy decision to make. In the end it was me who chose to walk away and close that door. I did so because I wasn't willing to pay that price. I wasn't willing to walk away from Orthodoxy. I wasn't willing to compromise or deny the convictions of my faith and I wasn't willing to settle for good when I know God wants to give me His best.

In that moment of decision to end this relationship, I had peace that I had made the right decision. I knew that in making that decision I needed to follow through and fully commit to the Lord through becoming rooted in Orthodoxy. Although I knew this and had spent years learning about the Orthodox faith I still delayed making that commitment. I still wrestled with God in my heart. There was this fear griping me, paralyzing me from moving forward in obedience to the Lord's leading. I was battling the same fears I have battled with my entire life. The fear of making a mistake, of being unworthy, of failing, of letting people down. The fear of becoming too settled, of being trapped. Looking back now of course it all seems a bit absurd, and completely unfounded. Yet that is often the case with fear.

So while everything seemed fine on the outside, inside I was in a constant battle with my thoughts and fears. In that battle with fear I was so grateful for the friendships God had given me. For being able to spend my Saturday's going to Church with friends. Having these amazing conversations and feeling so refreshed at the end of the day. Yet inside I was that little girl, so afraid of losing control, so afraid of making a mistake. As though if I became rooted I would miss out on some greater opportunity. Or once I became rooted and truly happy with my life, something would happen to take it all away.

I was afraid of becoming rooted. I have always been afraid of becoming rooted. In my mind rooted meant being stuck, trapped somewhere you didn't want to be. I have never allowed myself to become too settled or attached. It always seems that when I think things are going well and I am content with my life, something happens. I find myself suffering or facing an unexpected transition. So when I found myself in this season of life where things were absolutely wonderful. Where I feel so loved and blessed. Where I have a cozy beautiful home and a job I love. Where I am surrounded by wonderful friends, and have finally found a Coptic Orthodox Church community where I felt welcome. Where I felt wanted and where I can truly see myself being a part of the community. Fear gripped me even stronger. I was even more afraid to put down roots.

After ending things with this guy and attending this new Coptic Orthodox Church for a couple of months, I began praying for peace and courage to walk in full obedience. That is when I felt the Lord telling me to start writing this book. Start recording your journey of faith. Remind yourself of My faithfulness and Hand upon your life. Around this same time I had a visit from Abouna, just to talk and find out where I was at. Where I saw myself going within the Church and what was holding me back from becoming Orthodox. I obviously have had years of exposure to Orthodoxy and had been attending this new Church for several months now, so it made sense for him to ask these questions of me. Though I was really nervous about that visit. It was very intimidating for me to host Abouna. I wasn't sure what to expect or where the conversation would lead.

However, it was't as uncomfortable as I had expected. I found him much easier to talk with than I thought I would. In fact I was very encouraged, as well as challenged by our conversation. He brought up the subject of being rooted, which unbeknownst to him was exactly what I was wrestling with. He asked what was holding me back, why was I unsure? However, the thing that moved me the most, was at the end of our conversation. He said he would not push the topic again, that he was leaving it completely in my hands.

Something about that simple declaration, brought me so much peace. I don't know if it was because it made me feel that I was in control of the decision. Or if it was because there was no pressure on me to make a decision. I honestly think I had gotten to a point where I was over thinking things. I had allowed fear to hold me captive, and I was feeling so much pressure from all of my wonderful Coptic Orthodox friends to become Orthodox. I also felt as though I had let you all down because I hadn't come to a decision fast enough. It was this absurd circle of thought that lead me nowhere. Then somehow in Abouna's statement, that he was leaving it for me to decide if and when I became Orthodox, I found peace. So I decided to devote Lent to praying into this commitment. Not so much, should I become Orthodox. It was more about prayers for courage to step out in faith to become Orthodox.

It was also during this time that I dove into writing this book. This was something I had always thought about doing and even attempted to a few times. However, it was clear that this was finally the right season in my life for this project to come together. As I have worked on each chapter God has been moving in me, strengthening my faith, challenging me to be vulnerable. To overcome my fears of failure, unworthiness and so much more. Through sharing my journey of faith God has brought me greater clarity, and peace. He has granted me the courage to walk in obedience to the truth He has revealed to me, by stepping out and becoming Orthodox. He has given me courage to become deeply rooted in my faith and in doing so partake more fully of the abundant life He provides for His children. He is leading me into yet another chapter of my journey with Him. Although I have not conquered every fear, or overcome every struggle, I know that He will continue His faithfulness. I know He will continue to guide me each step of the way, and so I put my trust in Him and embrace the road ahead.

Psalm 9:10 *"And those who know your name put their trust in you, for you, O, LORD, have not forsaken those who seek you."*

www.ingramcontent.com/pod-product-compliance
Lightning Source LLC
Chambersburg PA
CBHW071928290426
44110CB00013B/1527